She Was, She Is

A book by David Ainsworth Cook

John Donne, "The Relic" --

"All measure, and all language, I should pass,

Should I tell what a miracle she was."

"Children and Art", <u>Sunday in the Park with George</u>, Stephen

Sondheim and James Lapine:

"There she is, there she is, there she is..."

Chapter One

This Is Not the End

This is not the end.

I said so myself as I bounded up the escalator in the mall bookstore. The north Georgia sun followed me in through the glass front windows and the panes of the wood door, past the kiosk and the information desk and halfway to the second floor, where I knew Karen was waiting in the café. Why was she waiting? She was waiting – and I was waiting with her, for the bookstore to text me to tell me I could then have the book that I had actually bought half an hour earlier. They made me buy it online, there in the store, even though I had the book in my hand at the cash register in front of the manager.

The north Georgia sun was too bright and too hot in late summer to wait around outdoors and the humidity was too high to want to sweat around a crowded mall, pacing as we waited for a text message – that's right, a text message giving me permission to pick up the book they had me buy online there in the mall store. Maybe this is the end of brick and mortar bookstores.

I could see Karen sitting alone at the little table, engaged with her smartphone, preoccupied. She was dressed in blue jeans, a sweater, with a scarf over her shoulders. On the table was a chai latte in a tall paper cup with a cardboard protector.

"There must be some way out of here," I said as I reached the table.

"Have they texted yet?" Karen asked, as I took a chair.

"No, they haven't. How long has it been?"

"We've been here nearly an hour. They told you it would take fifteen minutes and that was half an hour ago"

"Well, it all comes from what the cashier said, 'That's the only way you can get the website price, because they want you to use the web site.' So I did what they told me; and now we're waiting... and waiting."

The steaming espresso machine fizzed and some dishes and trays clattered. The hot aroma of fresh baked chocolate chunk cookies invaded the cool reconditioned air of the bookstore café near the section closest to the clearance table, partitioned by the island where they made the beverage concoctions.

I surveyed Karen, sitting studying her phone, and asked her, "Did you get over your embarrassment about wanting that book?"

"Don't you pick on me and call me fan-girl again. I know the book looks like fan fiction, but the author is well known, so it caught my eye."

Smiling, enjoying her indignation, I said, "I looked it up online and it had rave reviews, so I'll probably read it, too. Are you connected to the free Wi-Fi?" I pulled out my phone for the umpteenth time in less than an hour.

"Yes, but it's slow." She tapped her phone and shook it a little, as if that might help the connection.

"Well, waiting is partly my fault – I told you I'd buy the book for you; I mean, it was thirty percent off, but when I went to the cash register I found out that I couldn't get that price in the store even though it was on the bookstore's company web site. No, I had to log in on my phone, standing with the store manager, and pay by card online and then wait... wait for a text to tell me that I could actually have the book I was holding in my hand." I was exasperated all over again. "The manager even took the book away from me."

I drummed my fingers on the table. "I felt like a child when she took my book."

"I wonder what they would have done if you had just walked out with the book as soon as you finished your online transaction. Would they would accuse you of shoplifting? Of stealing the book you had just purchased?"

Karen shifted in her chair, "Can we talk about something else?"

"Any minute with you means talking." I waited for Karen to present a new topic; I reckoned she must have one since she initiated a change of topic. But, sitting in silence waiting I asked her, "What did you do today? What have the kids told you today?"

Karen didn't seem to hear that; instead she asked me, "What were you talking about in the car earlier, before we walked in here?"

"Oh... I was talking about The Four Horsemen of the Apocalypse. I was saying that I wondered if they were ancient auguries, and if prejudices against auguries, auspices, and astrology kept conservative Protestant people from being able to really interpret ancient texts."

Karen looked back down at her smartphone, obviously not engaged by that topic, then looked at me and said, "You know you're lucky." And kept looking as if she was studying me.

I waited, expecting more.

"You're lucky that people call you and ask you what you think. People call you or stop you and want to know your opinion on sundry things. They call you up and ask what you think about things and how they can do them. I think I do a good job. I've directed and started five or six programs and organizations, I'm directing one now, but people don't call me."

She shifted a little in her chair, set her phone on the table, took a sip from her chai latte, then continued: "I mean, I've started a literacy organization, directed volunteers, started an AmeriCorps program, run this and that, and now I'm directing a pastor search and hiring program. All of those had Director in the title... but no one calls me to ask how they should do things. I guess they think that what happens just happens and isn't it nice, and I just happen to be there. When they call they just want an update on the form they filled out online and they want to know if there has been any progress. Anything happen? What have you done? That's all."

Karen did not appear visibly moved but I was stunned.

7

Karen, not leaving a vacuum said, "This is ridiculous! We've been waiting around for 45 minutes already. By the time you get that book it will have been an hour... and it was one you picked up right here off a table in the store."

"You know," I interjected, "I'm not so much troubled by that anymore as I am by what you just said. I'm thinking of how you get calls all day from six children. They want to know what you think. And I know the team where you work discuss things with you at the office. I know people ask you to write their documents, wordsmith their grant proposals, launch their projects, and assemble their teams. Are you saying that you don't feel valued or perhaps don't feel fully utilized or maximized?"

"No, but they don't ask me the bigger questions, they don't ask me opinion questions. They ask how specific things are going, like 'Did that church get back to you? What do we need for this grant? Has Topeka responded yet?' What they don't come back with is 'Hey, Karen, what do you think are some of the problems going on here? What are your observations?' No, they ask specifics.

They don't seek my consultation. You're lucky because people seek out your experience and expertise, and they ask you what you think."

I looked at her, as if puzzled about that.

We were both entering our sixties, what some people would call "senior" and others might call "middle-aged". Karen looks younger than I do, more than two years younger; she recently turned sixty but she doesn't look it. "Girl" would seem like the right term for her, like an Irish girl, or a Scottish girl amid the heather. Dark chestnut hair. A nut brown maiden. Only fifty minutes earlier in the mall we had passed by one of those kiosk hawkers standing at a cart between stores who called out rather cattily, "Don't let your skin go!" as we passed by and Karen wryly through pursed lips said under her breath, "Do I look like I have?"

No, she doesn't. She never has, and she's proud of it, skin that's as smooth and fresh as milk, and hazel eyes that are sometimes blue.

"I'm going to write a book about you," I told her.

Karen kept looking at her phone and didn't look up when I said that. Why should she believe an off-hand promise like that?

This wasn't the end, still no text message, still couldn't have the book I paid for which was tucked away somewhere downstairs while we waited in the store. We were going to be there anyway waiting while our daughter Adrienne worked with her math tutor there in the cafe, but such considerations did not mitigate the annoyance of how the bookstore was treating us about that book.

The director of a search program that connects hundreds of pastors with hundreds of small searching churches was sitting across from me, and she said that people don't really consult her or seek her out. Is it because she is a woman? I've been annoyed over the years that men with MBA degrees could walk into a room and be offered fine jobs at good salaries with no more evidence of their worth than their appearance and their claim of a degree but she had to be something like an entrepreneur, creating a job for herself and selling its value to a potential hire, even though she had the same degree, from a good school, and a proven record of value.

Karen looked up from her phone, sipped her chai latte and added, "I don't mean to say that no one talks to me. Don't take it like that; it just seems like no one calls me directly; they fill out a form on the web site and then I contact them. No one asks me what I think, not on the broader issues, not until there is a project, you know, like the grant, and then we work on that and there is a lot of talking. They call me in and ask, 'Karen, what do you think? How can we make this work?' But do they call and ask why something didn't work? But people call you and ask you where you think things are going and how can they set up their project and make it work. That's what I would like to talk about, where I think things are going, what would I envision and how would I launch it. More than thirty years, more than half a dozen organizations, most of them I started from scratch. Grant writing. Assembling boards. Partnering with organizations. Getting one organization to form a new partnership with another. I want something I can build. I want something to sink my teeth into, something that I know will work if we'll just make it."

Karen drank her chai latte. "I like your coffee better."

I take her coffee every morning. And I hand her laptop computer to her while she's still lying in bed. I do it every morning because I love her and I want her day to start nicely. She has to go to work every day. No one knows who said it first, but there's a saying, 'Be kind because everyone you meet is fighting a hard battle.' It's become a meme, you know, and a Tweet. We've had a lot of hard battles, and climbed a lot of mountains. Some people have died along the way. I'm hoping I remember to write about them. Making a pot of coffee, and carrying a cup upstairs are easy.

We married in December 1979. We had been married 39 years, sitting there in that bookstore, drinking chai latte and waiting for a text to tell us we could have the book I paid for half an hour earlier, and waiting on our fifth daughter, our sixth child, who would be our eighth child but we lost two in miscarriages.

Eight... I tell you, there have been trials and there have been battles, some of them sad and some of them lonely and most of them unnoticed. Some where you really don't know the answers.

You should see this woman at home, in her own space; next to her on the floor beside our bed are so many cords and wires on so many papers and letters, piled and snaked and stacked that they're either going to catch fire and burn up the house one day or I am going to trip and break my neck. She is the manager, bill payer, tax accountant, utility and property manager, advisor, consultant, correspondent, fan fiction reader, blog responder, travel planner... director. So there are myriad sticky notes, post-it notes, bits, papers, folders, memo pads, legal pads, journals, address books, and pens and pencils, and paper clips, and phone chargers, and those multi-plug outlet things to prevent a short – surge protectors, that's what they're called... and a table and a lamp and her phone and her Kindle. Maybe "no one calls" but there are some ways that millions of words and numbers get transmitted. That they find their way to the right place in a dizzying array is an acrobatic or juggling feat that is as bewildering and astonishing as an aerial dogfight above a World War I battlefield. And how, amid all that, has she read and kept up with all those fictional characters and story arcs and trends and discussion groups and comments and the kaleidoscopes and the cascades and the crashing cymbals and the sounds of tympanies?

I get fatigue. 'Decision fatigue,' my son calls it. The kids don't like it if I look tired or fatigued when they talk to me but I can't help it. Look at her; somehow, at approximately the right time each morning, Karen throws lunch together and a salad in Tupperware and heads off to work, leaving at around 9:00 when she's due at 9:00. 'It takes seventeen minutes to get there, I've timed it,' I say. I think I started carrying coffee to her every day only about four years ago. One teaspoon of sugar, some low-fat light vanilla creamer, in a substantial mug. She likes the mug I bought that has fish on it. Sometimes all six kids call and text at once.

There was an old woman that lived in a shoe, she had so many children she didn't know what to do. Not this one – who is not old.

"We're really blessed," Karen says. "Did you see the clip of Sarah Lambert singing and playing guitar? Did you see Julianne's Instagram? The grandbaby is running. Did you watch him kick that ball? Anna Lara is doing so well with yoga."

A daughter in Germany. A daughter in Seattle. A daughter in India. International travel. Skype. Facetime. And a call at 6:00 a.m. is because that's 3:30 p.m. in India. God, can I never sleep? One daughter has been to an Ivy League college. Another daughter is at the second oldest university in the nation; even if you say 'it's not Ivy League', it is designated as 'a public ivy'. Five have been to colleges and universities, two large state and private universities. Three state champions in speaking, forensics and debate. One Governor's Honors. A daughter on a fencing team. A daughter in Air Force ROTC.

"No one ever calls and asks about parenting, either. I guess I don't fit the picture they want. Just like I'm at the mall here but not shopping. I'm just not the stereotype."

Maybe that stereotype is a product of affluence, which we don't seem to be part of. A director of nonprofits and a college art teacher... The pastor of the church we attend in suburbia said, aghast in stunned awe, 'Do you know that there are people in our community who qualify for free or reduced lunch? Their kids in the schools?' He meant it compassionately; he had no idea that we spent many years in that economic bracket. For 19 years we qualified as a statistic in the counties we lived in as 'low income' with the kids eligible for free and reduced lunch at the public schools, from the time our first one entered private preschool (the private preschool didn't operate in the county adjustment ratio), until sometime in the past few years here when our salaries finally elevated us out of the lowest economic bracket. The first year we moved here to Georgia a school teacher called to ask when and where they could deliver the charity parcels because we still qualified for reduced price lunch. That couldn't have been more than ten years ago. Managing low income might be more difficult than managing wealth. Why had we been like that? The double whammy of a woman in non-profit management and an art teacher. The part of that equation I was thinking of at the moment was the unfair decision to give a woman in nonprofit organizations such lower salaries. The basic stereotype there had to do with her being a woman.

Around us, in that bookstore café, were unnoticed dozens of other conversations, the squeals of the machines that heated water for the hot beverages, the aromas of pumpkin, spices, and coffee mingled with the fragrances of new books, the scratch of chairs pushed on tile floors, and sounds of smartphones, but there was still no bleeping permission text. We still couldn't have that book. We were still waiting.

My smartphone trumpeted like a fox horn.

"Hi, Nathan," I said into the phone; and to Karen I said in aside, "It's Nathan. He says that he's actually in the parking lot just below us, about to leave because he had in the past few minutes gotten off work at the restaurant next door." To Nathan, into the phone, I said, probably louder than necessary, "We're upstairs, waiting for a book; come up and join us and I'll tell you the whole story of The Wait for the Book."

Enter Nathan, in his black uniform clothes and shoes, a restaurant logo in red on his sleeve. As he sprang upstairs and strolled to the table we told him the story about that book and the text message we were waiting for and we all laughed. What absurdity! Our little intimate bookstore box theatre of the absurd.

As I said to Nathan, "I mean, how can you be so controlled by a retailer over a book you actually paid for that you have to keep sitting in a chair in a store waiting for a text message to tell you that you can now have the book that you had to hand over half an hour earlier? It has worked out pretty well for them: while we've been waiting I bought nine things from the seventy-five percent off clearance table, two beverages, and a new book online, all while being trapped here for an hour. 'I wouldn't lose a friend over a book,' Denys Finch Hatton said, but they did."

Just then my phone trumpeted again, that time with a text from the bookseller informing me that I could now have the book I already purchased, saying it had arrived when I knew damn well it arrived because I handed it over more than half an hour earlier and watched a manager set it behind a register downstairs. Ugh. But... cheers! We had the text at last! Now we could be free!

We collected Adrienne who had finished her tutoring session, proceeded down the escalator (does going down make it a "de-escalator"?), picked up the onerous book, and exited together out to the last golden rays of summer sun, laughing.

It seemed like I ought to hear a narrator or director say, "Dim the lights. Cue the music."

But it still isn't the end.

Chapter Two

Karen awoke at 2:30 a.m. What was unusual was that she stayed awake.

"What happened, sweetheart? Did something scare you?"

"No, no, I wasn't scared, but I couldn't stop thinking. I had to sort it all out. I was trying to make sense of the arc of you and me and all our kids over the past ten years, to get the trajectories all together in my mind so I would know where everyone is and where everyone is going."

Six children, teenage to thirty, two sons-in-law, a grandchild, and a fiancé... that was all she was trying to sort out. Sure... no problem...

"I'm trying to make sense of all of it so that I can be settled with it."

She was still bundled up in quilt and bedspread, in a comfy nightgown, with her laptop on a tray across her legs, her Kindle next to her, her phone on the nightstand under the little brass lamp she has treasured since childhood, and across her ankles was the large sketchbook I had given her, open to pages with lines and names written on them, and I leafed through those, page after page, of what were obviously timelines and charts in pencil.

Rain pelted on the skylight like impatiently drumming fingers. There were aromas of candles from the hall. On the floor beside the bed, the cords, books, notebooks, bits of paper, and other litter that Karen usually had strewn there, next to pillows and scarves and stray socks.

So, at 2:30 a.m. she drew a timeline across many sheets of paper, starting ten years back and placing each person and their moves on that line.

"This was just something I had to do. It's difficult to hold in my head a picture of where everyone was at one moment. I don't always think in words; I think in pictures. I had to keep it visual; that's why I had to draw it."

I couldn't picture it, in the early morning dark, as I brought her first cup of coffee. She had already been awake three hours. The aroma of fresh espresso coffee and vanilla creamer spread comfortably through the dark, as the rain continued to drum.

Pictures of timelines in her head? I tried to imagine it in words.

Does anyone think in words? I mean, actually see and read words in their mind? Or do we all hear voices, like narrating our thoughts? Sometimes I've got Roger Livesey narrating and sometimes Emma Thompson is talking, explaining things to me; it just seems to come naturally to hear someone else tell me what I'm thinking, they very often say it better. At least it sounds better when they say things; perhaps it's the music of their voices that is better. I know I've read books in dreams, and seen printed instructions and recognized signs in dreams, but Karen has said that she sees time and memories differently than I do. She sees what is in her head like the timeline she was drawing.

Perhaps she was working through other things in her mind and they welled up in her sleep.

She has been memorizing John Donne's "A Valediction Forbidding Mourning". We were talking about that at the table yesterday. Some of those stanzas get tricky because the poem is written as if Donne was mixing some ingredients, like alchemy – of course, he wrote another poem titled, "Love's Alchemy", but let's stay away from that one, it seems a bit misogynistic at the end – in "A Valediction" it's as if he was making something mechanical, the mechanism of compass dividers on a map. You have to remember all those pieces and parts – eyes, lips, hands, and touching and "care to miss" – and the elements like "gold to airy thinness beat", to get the mixture, to get the parts and put it together.

She was mapping time and life and all the pieces and parts of her family at 2:30 a.m., drawing them out on a timeline, like laying out a strategy or a road or, as she said, "a trajectory", trying to put it all together into one thing.

"I have to get a grip on the trajectories of the people I love. If I had them all in one room then I could see them and I would know they were here and safe. Anybody knows how good that feels, to have everyone at home for a holiday, all in one room, all under one roof, together and safe. It's having a connection with them all at once, to know where all of them are, and to feel good about them.

"I was trying to make sense of where everyone is going so that I can be settled with it, so I can be connected to them. With only one it would be easy, but trying to think of and follow all of them at once was impossible. I had to bring them all together in one place. It was very unsettling that I didn't automatically know, that I couldn't see it, I had to think it through and I had to make something so that I could see it."

"You didn't have any coffee last night did you?" I asked. "Or ice cream? I mean, was it just your thoughts that woke you up? Were you anxious about anything?"

"No, no, and no, I wasn't worried about anything, I just started trying to picture everyone's path and I couldn't see it all together, so I got frustrated and I couldn't stop thinking about it. That's why I had to sit up and draw it out.

"But I couldn't start at 'now', in the present, I had to go back through the past, so I went back ten years to when we all moved, when we moved from Kansas to Georgia and Sarah Lambert and Anna Lara were away at colleges. I was trying to track where everybody had been, and how they intersected."

Karen had to look backward to find the arcs to see the path of the present. Things became confusing when people started branching off, and she had to see those branches, how and when they happened, and see where everyone was at the time, leading to the present moment, and the connections. She had to examine things by walking backward through the past, to find the arcs of their trajectories and follow them to the present. That way she kept a grip on it. That way she kept grounded.

She had to have a road map. She had to see their trajectories. It wasn't enough just to think about it, she had to see first, and then save it in her head. She had to go to the past to find the present.

"Then all the tricky parts lined up."

You know, I don't think like that, but I do occasionally examine the map of the solar system. I draw things like that about the planets and the constellations and the stars, and I will look at web sites that have animations that show the movements of the planets backwards through years and years. I wondered if I would be a problem at the Jet Propulsion Laboratory as they tried to study a near-Earth pass by an asteroid, because I would start wondering about all the other objects and if or when each one might be in danger of colliding with another, and wondering if that one that was struck by chance could then carom to Earth. Maybe it wasn't heading toward Earth before and no one was worried about it, but then a chance bank shot sent it plummeting. Do they play pool at NASA?

Scanning and studying the connectedness of things moving through space and time.

I admit it, I'm often surprised by connections. Serendipity and chance encounter, a surprise revelation, a startling realization, all those things seem to keep me in a constant state of wonder.

Not Karen, she expected them. Her response to what surprised me was more like, "Right. Yep. I expected that. I knew that had to be there."

"I'm always looking for how things relate," she would say. "I am looking for pattern and purpose. What did those people in the past do? How did they live? How do we relate to it?"

That must be why she liked to go to museums and historic places.

Even the time I discovered the engraved handprint among the Native American petroglyphs, the one no one else had seen

27

before, and my twisted fingers matched it, she acted like she had expected to find it. She didn't say that, but her air and what she did say seemed like, "Well of course, I expected to find that there."

Was the pattern of our life imprinted back there in the pattern of the past? Or was that trail or thing we found just a pattern to meditate upon like the one on the floor of Chartres Cathedral?

That path in Chartres did not seem like it would get you anywhere. I know, you are supposed to get to the center and have a realization, or perhaps work out a few things along the way. Karen would want to go somewhere. She wouldn't just want to walk, she would want to have a direction and walk with a purpose. There has to be a destination. Walk with confidence. I know what I'm doing. I know where I'm going.

"That's how you walked when I first saw you," she told me. "I was looking out my dorm window and I watched you. You knew where you were going, like you knew what you were doing. You moved that way. Your body conveyed that. You had a purpose and a plan and a destination. I could see it."

Keep moving. Keep walking. Forward motion. Know where you're going. Just keep moving on.

I was surprised when Karen told me that she liked to watch me fly fishing. I've never been able to get her to go fishing, but she said that she liked to watch me fishing.

"It's really enjoyable to watch someone who knows what they're doing, who planned and prepared. You would go from one place to another, like stations, and you would know just where and how to cast – watching the arc of the cast and seeing the placement of that lure. It's impressive.

"I like to watch soccer," that shocked everyone. No... "I like international soccer much more than American football. I mean, in football a play is over in a second and then they have to draw lines on the screen and explain what just happened, but it's over. When they are playing soccer the teams move around the field and they seem to lead each other this way and that."

Kind of like watching Border Collies lead sheep.

"Oh, yes! I love to watch Border Collies! There's a beauty to a movement like that."

Speaking of moves, we've moved to quite a number of places. Los Angeles. Papua New Guinea. Virginia. From Virginia we moved to Alabama, then North Carolina, then way out west to Kansas, and from Kansas we moved to Georgia, always in pursuit of purpose, usually a better job, higher pay, better benefits.

Packing up and unpacking. Boxing and unboxing. Then we have to unwrap and search for things. We had lived another year in yet another rented house and we still had not unboxed some things. We were digging the other night in some boxes trying to find the small objects that used to sit in the wot-not and curio. Searching for this, searching for things from the past.

"Where are the seashells? The Wentletraps and the green snails?" We untangled handfuls of brown packing paper to find tin soldiers and porcelain maidens, glass swans and my old Egyptian cigarette lighter.

"Here they are!"

The creamy white spirals of the Precious Wentletraps and the small green cones of the Manus snails from Papua New Guinea.

"And here is Mister Ford's elephant," the little ceramic coin bank with a blue blanket over its back that said "Germany".

We've had to do some driving – sometimes panicked driving – to get back to a place to find something that was lost. We couldn't find Teddy, Sarah Lambert's teddy bear, after a camping trip, when she was in grade school. We had been camping in Florida and were leaving to head for home when she realized in the car that Teddy was missing. Oh the heartache! The fear and worry! Teddy was like the sixth child at that time, like part of the family; she had held him and taken him everywhere since she was one year old. We turned around, drove back to Florida and searched the campground. We called people – that was using payphones back then – and we had just about initiated local search when we decided to unpack everything. Teddy was rolled up in the sleeping bag! Oh joy! So what if we were going to be traveling three or four hours later than we planned? We had found Teddy.

Years later, we left Dollah, Julianne's doll, at a motel in Helen, Georgia. Fortunately the housekeeper had taken care of it and the front desk was holding her, but it meant a four-hour roundtrip to go back, get Dollah, maybe eat something, and then go back home. A lonely trip, too, because it had to be the next day, Monday, with kids in school and Karen at her office. Fortunately I had a "holiday" that day and could go get Dollah.

Ten, maybe fifteen years ago, Karen gave me a list as a present. I can't remember if it was for Valentine's Day or our wedding anniversary or a birthday present, she had put together a concise sequential chronological list of all that had happened in our lives together since our wedding. She was very pleased and proud of it, and I was quite happy and grateful to get it. It would have taken me a lot more work, a lot more time and a lot of asking questions to put something like that together, but she does not remember in the same manner as I do, and she remembers a lot more.

I had to search for pictures of my mother to show to our youngest daughter, Adrienne. I knew I had them, I felt certain I could find them, so I had to search through boxes and folders and three-ring binders and USB drives until I found them, along with pictures of Karen's mother so that Adrienne could see her grandmothers.

Then I took photos of the photographs with my phone so that I could text them to Adrienne.

"I wish I could have known them!" Adrienne said, and she cried a few times like that, and Adrienne cried a few times reading this book that I promised Karen I would write -- a book about her so that other people could know her like I know her.

Why don't they know you like I know you? Why don't they see what I see?

A lot of time last year was taken up planning for a trip to Scotland as a gift for Karen's sixtieth birthday. She is usually in on the planning for surprising someone else, a thing she loves to do, but this time she was in on the "surprise" for herself so that she could be sure to do all the things that she had wanted to do and dreamed of doing for years.

"We have to know where we're going."

And she got quite angry and offended when she thought that I was not taking part in the planning! She disagrees, she was concerned by what seemed to be my disinterest. We got there and back and we saw everything we meant to see, so let's not quibble about past planning, that's what I say.

Our oldest daughter, Sarah Lambert the artist, had been to Scotland with her husband, Jordan. They had been to Dunkeld and Birnam Wood, walked around the Hermitage, and been to Clava

34

Cairns, and they told us about places and had suggestions. Anna Lara, number two child, had been to Scotland on her honeymoon with her husband, Vashisht. She also had suggestions, and they took the lead in planning our travel.

Sarah Lambert studied the Neolithic prehistoric sites, the cairns and stone circles, and she was fascinated by Paleolithic cave paintings and wanted to visit the ones in France, such as Lascaux and Chauvet. You could crawl among the rocks of the cairns in Scotland, but they won't let you crawl through the caves in France anymore, that did too much damage. You have to be satisfied with videos and books and virtual recreations where they have them. Perhaps with her archaeology degree and credentials they may let her get up close and personal, nose to nose one day with those bears and bulls and lions in the dark.

I don't know... my professor card didn't get me in to see the Worthies in Heidelberg.

Sarah Lambert paints, she paints watercolors of maps and caves and trees like the giant Birnam Oak that Shakespeare may have seen and we saw. She paints and charts the stars.

Transparent blues and blue-violets, the warm umber and rose

madder and the colors of wood like veins of Van Dyke brown,

spaces and shapes that map the world and space and time.

Sarah Lambert wants to connect with the ancient past.

"Did you find what you were looking for?" I asked Karen.

"Yes," she said, and smiled as she squeezed my hand, one

of those "I did it, I got it" squeezes with a little backward shake, as

if she'd just won some points in a game.

"I just had to have them all together. I had to see them all

at once. I had to have their arcs and their trajectories. I had to

know where they were going."

Does there always have to be a purpose?

"Sometimes the purpose is just walking. Walking is good for

your health. It's good to walk. Keep to the path and keep moving."

Do you always have to know something, regain something?

"Sometimes it's just the process that matters. I couldn't sleep until I'd done it. I had to take that time and lay it out and see it. Once I had done that I felt better and I could rest.

"But I go in expecting to find it. Sometimes I expect to find it ready, but it isn't always ready, and then I have to work and get it right."

Through the doors and this way, in the hallways of the mind. No, that would be my way, or a way, but that's not her way.

Pull on it and stretch it out, the panels that connect, the panoply of time.

If you're talking of parades, they're somewhere else. This path is taken.

"Can we talk some more?" I ask, because I have a lot of questions.

Chapter Three

Scotland

I've been listening over and over to "She's a Rainbow" by The Rolling Stones. When I told Karen I was listening to The Rolling Stones to make me happy she made an unpleased face. The Rolling Stones... aren't they Satanic? We don't listen to them do we? So I played several not so satanic sounding Rolling Stones songs and she changed her mind.

Her world is full of music. She wanted to major in music performance in college – performance, mind you, not theory – she plays piano – and her memory is filled with folk songs, like the ones Granny taught her and the Scottish folk songs that we have sung many times.

Karen wanted to go to Scotland for her sixtieth birthday, and the kids conspired together and treated her to a trip. We are working our way backward through time, to the past, you see.

She wanted to go to Scotland, but I wanted to go to England. She had never been to Scotland and had always wanted to go, even since she was a little girl, but I wanted to go to Manchester and from there to Bolton and Bury in search of my ancestors. Little did I know that ancestors aplenty were waiting for us in Scotland, but I should have guessed it. She prevailed. We went to Scotland (and a bit of England to see Hadrian's Wall in The Border Lands).

Months and weeks of planning. Hours and hours and maps of planning for her special sixtieth birthday trip. I had a special treat for my sixtieth birthday the year before. They took me by surprise to Gatlinburg, Tennessee, which has always been one of my favorite places. I have a deep affection for it because it is where I met Jesus when I was sixteen years old. After this last trip, though, when leaving Gatlinburg, I thought about the dyslexic devil worshippers who sold their souls to Santa. There were t-shirts and billboards there with his name and face.

I knew what a trip to Scotland would mean: two weeks of me driving on the left, which meant sitting on the right while she sat screaming on the left, "Look out! You're too close! Watch out on the left! There's a bridge! Oh gosh! Oh gosh!" She took to reading aloud what Siri was saying at the same time Siri said it, which reminded me of Sigourney Weaver in *Galaxy Quest* who was constantly echoing the spaceship computer, so I said, "You've got one job on this ship, it's a stupid one, but you're going to do it."

I'm not saying that Karen is a bad passenger, just because she tries to squeeze up in her seat as if she could make herself and the car fit through the single lane bridges better, or because she works an invisible brake pedal in the passenger floor board, or because she grips a handle in the door as if collision is imminent. No, she's a good driving companion. She just starts yelling in the dark tunnel, "Your lights, David! Turn on your lights!" forgetting that she's wearing sunglasses.

To prepare for the trip meant I had to lose fifteen pounds and be able to walk five or six miles at a stretch. Five or six miles aren't too many, they only take two hours of walking at my three miles per hour pace. Most of those would be uphill, of course, like walking up and down the Royal Mile in Edinburgh, multiple times, the full length of it, from palace to castle, and then up to Arthur's Seat George Bridge back to The Royal Mile. Arthur's Seat. Like walking up Dollar Glen, along the craggy stream, up steps and steps, hundreds of steps, to Campbell castle. Or walking down and up and up and down The Falls of Foyer, with its pebbly paths and wet rails. Uphill. Over hill. Sometimes in the rain. Wet. I swear there is a section of Edinburgh called Dean Village that is like an M.C. Escher engraving and is all uphill. Don't go there at the end of a weary day. If you get down there you still have to get back up, and it's all uphill.

There is no way to go on a trip with Karen and not have to walk up miles of mountains, even if you're injured. She once made me walk up Stone Mountain in Georgia the day after I had fallen down a flight of stairs and thought I had broken my back.

We're going on a trip? There must be mountains.

She planned our trip with amazing knowledge, detail and precision, a lifetime of studied longing projected into road maps and choices of sights to see.

We were going to go to Scotland by way of Ireland. My advice – and I am going to insist on this from now on – is to not attempt to save money by taking layovers and changing flights; instead fly direct, make your air trip last only seven or eight hours at most, not become a 26-hour ordeal with two layovers in airports that aren't really interesting. We stopped over for five hours in Dulles airport. The architecture of Dulles thrilled me when I was a kid, but having passed through it too many times and once in a blizzard it isn't as exciting as it once seemed... besides, it has "dull" in the name. And no frills Aer Lingus is so no frill that they don't even open their desk and sometimes don't even have people to staff it. Twenty-six hours there. Twenty-six hours back. Twenty-six hours that should have only been eight at most. Three airplanes of decreasing size to get there. Three airplanes of moderately increasing size coming back. With no airplane or airport that offered any comfort.

Scotland in July was beautiful. It's a really nice section of North Carolina, it just takes longer to get there from here.

A lot of it really does seem exactly like parts of North Carolina, not so much the piedmont or the coast but the mountains and mountain trails and streams seem like places in Appalachia. The Tweed River at Peebles in England reminded me of Oconaluftee at Cherokee and other places in the Smoky Mountains where we've camped and fished, even down to the way people accessed and played in the river. There were changing booths near the river downtown in Peebles. Dollar Glen and the Falls of Foyer in Scotland could easily have been in the Appalachian Mountains of North Carolina. Cascading water over mossy rocks, dark shady trails with tall trees. Scotland was once part of North America, after all, on the same tectonic plate at the eastern edge of it. Perhaps

43

Scotland misses Appalachia, the way all Scots seem to yearn for Scotland. Alas, I suppose we're all suffering, always.

We spent the first few days of our time in Scotland in Edinburgh, which meant that I mercifully did not have to get into another vehicle or have to drive yet. I just had to walk uphill – a paved hill, but a hill. Along the Royal Mile we went into some of my favorite pubs and churches and castles that I ever visited – and I would say that same praise about the whole of Scotland and about that whole trip.

In the pubs, like World's End and Tolbooth Tavern, and Ryrie's in Haymarket, they served Belhaven's Best ale. That was astonishing. The name astonished me, it took me aback. Belhaven. I grew up in a neighborhood called Belhaven. The first twenty-three years of my life were in Belhaven. Karen and I met at Belhaven College. We walked hand in hand around Belhaven. The name Belhaven follows me everywhere I go or I encounter it in every greeting... and here in the pubs of Scotland was a creamy dark beer named Belhaven. I asked if I could buy the pint glasses with "Belhaven's Best" printed on the glass and suddenly became a local hero as One Honest Man. "Most people just nick those – steal them – and you actually asked to buy it! Here, you can have two! And here's a Strongbow glass for the lady." We tipped generously.

About the pubs: World's End with its dark wood interior, almost black, is a bit narrow for a broad shouldered bloke, divided between bar and dining, as some of the pubs were. Great food, warm and congenial hosts, it was one place that practically insisted that we try haggis – and the haggis was very good. After dinner they offered up hot chocolate cake bathed in hot fudge sauce that made the ideal accompaniment to a dram of Scotch. If you really want to enjoy Scotch whiskey, take a taste of dark chocolate with it.

Tolbooth Tavern is in the lower portion on The Mile, beyond World's End, not far from Parliament. It looks as if it was once a jeweler's or other merchant shop, not like its namesake the ancient prison. Charming and quaint exterior, the lush purple of its upper deck dining is about as Victorian as you could find. Fantastic food of portions too big for us but greatly appreciated. We could hear the excited conversations of the locals at the bar below, and once while we were there everyone suddenly rushed out of the place to the street, just outside the tavern door, where we joined the crowd as the royal guard bagpipes marched down the hill to Holyrood Palace. I love the sound of bagpipes, and they echoed off the buildings walling either side of the street and echoed above the crowd in the bright sun and warm July air. We revisited each of those pubs two or three times.

We found Ryrie's by chance in Haymarket in a quest for a pub with Belhaven's Best. Its blue accented exterior almost matches the old rail station or an exchange house of some kind. Great service, and a nice menu for the end of a weary day, it obviously has a regular clientele.

The churches and the abbeys, such as St. Giles and Greyfriars and St. Mary's, were pleasant and spacious. In St. Mary's there was a copy of the order to execute Charles I; I'm sure it's just a facsimile copy, with its signatures on parchment and ribbons and

46

red seals. It was a convincing facsimile and fascinating to see. There were details to marvel at such as the thistles in the windows of St. Giles – and the statue of Bobby on the street at Greyfriars that made you feel instantly like a Scottish national and a local and as if you would become forever sentimental over all of it. As if the folk songs didn't make us emotional and sentimental enough. Those will make you mourn and become homesick for people you never knew and places that were never your home, as if they were your own.

John Knox's House was there, along the Royal Mile. It juts out at an angle, making the sidewalk wider at its place. All in the same brownish gray dun color stone that characterizes all of The Royal Mile, perhaps all of the old city of Edinburgh.

John Knox's House was a museum, just around the corner from our flat. I didn't want to visit John Knox's House and Karen didn't either, but we did. It was only five pounds entrance fee and it gave us a lot to talk about, mainly what was Knox's wrong view about the gospel. That's why we didn't want to visit it. I can't seem to escape Presbyterianism, a lifetime of it from grade school through college, through sometimes preaching, and there wouldn't be a Presbyterian without Knox. Give him his credit and his due, but with some things I don't always agree.

In Knox's teaching, you had to suffer to be worthy of the gospel. In other words, you had to work and sacrifice and suffer to be deserving. No, that's wrong, that's not the gospel. The good news of the gospel is that Jesus chooses you and saves you freely and that's what makes you worthy, not by anything that you have done. Because He deserves it you have salvation. Can we please get rid of the words "worthy" and "deserving"? They should be discarded along with "conservative".

But there is a charm to Edinburgh and everything in it, and the charm of the place took hold of me, a quiet and studied calm that actually seemed oddly homey, and I found myself looking out onto the street from Knox's window, over his old desk, through its grid of small clear panes.

I took a picture through Knox's window and now I look through it every day as the wallpaper on my phone and laptop, looking up the Royal Mile, at the memories there.

Knox's house fascinated us for reasons other than his theology. We enjoyed the location because it had once been near The Netherbow, the gate and wall that used to be World's End on The Royal Mile. Some old maps of the world from centuries ago say, "Beyond this point there be dragons," and the Netherbow in Edinburgh must have held a similar mystique in The Middle Ages, as in "beyond this point ends the royal protection and the true religion," or something like that. World's End.

I think I saw "the end of the world" in Papua New Guinea, or somewhere in the South Pacific; it seems like there was a road sign or something there that said that. This World's End must have meant something else. Did they mean it globally? Perhaps in medieval times they meant it as reflecting on protection or the quality of life.

We are walking our way back through the past, as I said.

49

Karen stayed around the World's End, reading the informational signs posted along the walk, photographing the gold cobblestones among the gray ones that marked the footprints of the ancient gate. She wanted to dine in the World's End pub several times, and hovered around the corners, her imagination mesmerized by the thought of that old wall and gate and the crowds that wandered through it. What did they think back then? What did they really believe? We tried to imagine walking under the shadow of that gate.

From Edinburgh we went to other walls, Hadrian's Wall and Antonine's Wall. We went to the forts and communities that once existed along the wall: Vindolanda and Housesteads of Hadrian's Wall, and Rough Castle of Antonine's Wall. Karen had always wanted to walk on the wall. She got t-shirts that said, "I Walked the Wall". At Housesteads we walked atop it. It's a spectacular view. Someone was harvesting tall trees. The sky was blue and the grass was green. The exposed stones looked white in the summer sun. At Vindolanda Karen was interested in the museum as much as the wide array of ruins, and she attracted my

attention to the fragments of clothing archaeologists had found,

the weaves and colors the Romans had made. That way we were

with those people, those ancient Roman citizens along the far

western frontier of the islands, parents and grandparents, raising

children and grandchildren, educating them and passing along

traditions, generation after generation in their isolated outpost

that became their own remote culture and civilization there along

the wilderness far from Rome.

The landscape had her attention most. The mountains, the

hills, the views from the walls. She kept noticing the purple

foxgloves everywhere, Digitalis as she kept saying, like it was a well-

known secret and she whispered it with a knowing smile, a grin

playing at the corners of her mouth. That "ahem, see? I know that,"

air. So it became a thing for us to do to try to compose pictures

with foxgloves in the foreground. At the gray stone ruins of

Kilchurn Castle, where she tried to position herself in the grass and

weeds to get a picture of foxgloves in the foreground between herself and the castle, I yelled to some guy to get out of a window, out of the way, so she could take a picture. I'm glad that didn't lead to a fight. The big oaf in white, he just malingered in an arch staring dumbly at his phone until I yelled, "Get out of the window!" He was pretty good about it, I guess, he didn't hit me when we passed inside the ruins.

We stopped briefly in Kilchurn like we stopped briefly in Stirling like we stopped for just a minute in Loch Awe, because we were hurrying on our way to The Isle of Mull, passing through the sites of the folk songs we sang, the songs about Loch Tay and Killin (it sounds like "kay-lean" when you sing it as a child along with the Corries), going to Mull on our way in search of the places in the 1940 film *I Know Where I'm Going*, and from there to Iona, another place she had always wanted to see. Our Scottish folk song tour versus our quest for the settings of Powell and Pressburger movie tour – we actually spent a bit more time at Kilchurn than we did in some other places.

About Iona: Karen used to have an antique silver necklace of St. Michael's cross from Iona. She bought it on a trip to London as a teenager, a few years before we met in college. It was stolen when someone robbed our house while we were gone to our first daughter's wedding at Christmas, stolen along with a penny she had picked up off the floor of the restaurant on our first date. The thief must have dumped her jewelry box into a bag. How else or why else would he have taken that penny? We searched in the years since for another cross like that one, with the designs on both sides, but never found another. The cross has Bible story scenes carved on it, much the same way that the sarcophagus of Junius Bassus does, sermons in stones in the manner from the third century through the seventh one.

We were so intent on getting on the ferry to Mull that we missed out on Oban, one of our few regrets. But our minds and hearts were set for the island port of Tobermory. We felt about making it there about like our youngest, Adrienne, did when we passed under the gate at Walt Disney World. "I can't believe I'm here! I have a great family!" she said.

No amusement park could ever terrify me as much as those single lane roads and passing places, especially the roads to Moy Castle and Carsaig pier. "I can't believe you drove all those roads in one day! You Americans!" one woman said, impressed with our nerves. They were shaken, believe me, they were shaken. But we found the phone booth by the waterfall, ("It was a dry summer when they put it in. They forgot that when it rains...," I can hear Roger Livesey tell Wendy Hiller...) and we found Moy Castle, and the road, and the path, and the gate, both sites from the film, *I Know Where I'm Going*. It was dark and misty around Moy Castle, along the shore, a perfectly moody Scottish setting.

Our room looked out over The Western Isles Hotel and the blue waters of The Sound of Mull. We ate there, in The Western Isles, next to the Killoran Room, looking out at The Sound, thinking and talking about Killoran, the name of an island **and** a character in *I Know Where I'm Going*. Place and person were synonymous and interchangeable in that film, much like some things might seem to be in Scotland and in Appalachia, where person and place merge in identity and hearts' care. Karen has studied and studied the arrangement of that place. She wanted to know what was there in 1940 when they lensed *I Know Where I'm Going* compared to what we were seeing and walking among years later.

Part of our journey through Scotland was to find stone circles and standing stones, like the brooding setting of Clava Cairns and the odd Corrimony Cairn along the road not far from Urquhart Castle and Drumnadrochit. We really enjoyed Drumnadrochit, such a pleasant friendly relief after the crush and bustle of Urquhart Castle. If you like a pleasant, uncrowded, and more gracious experience when you travel, then I say by all means stop and linger in Drumnadrochit and no matter what anyone tells you or offers they make you should really avoid Urquhart Castle.

I found myself grieving for the young woman who was laid to rest in Corrimony Cairn, as if she had laid down to sleep an everlasting sleep. She must have been very special and much loved and they must have mourned and grieved over losing her, to lay her down so gently and tenderly and remember her that way. All these centuries perhaps millennia later just a stain remains, a shadow, but they'd recreated her, drawn a picture of her on the informative sign, and I grieved as if she had been my daughter or my mother. Who knows? Perhaps she was. The DNA results from 23andMe say that my ancestors were Gravettian, the cave painters and the makers of The Venus of Willendorf, and that my ancestry passed through Scotland. Perhaps these industrious people were my people. I know that Karen embraces them as hers, and that was why we were there.

Some of Karen's kin were Stewarts. She takes their histories personally. At an exhibit case in Fort William Karen revisited the story of Alan Breck Stewart. The West Highland Museum had the murder weapon from The Appin Murder and a copy of Stevenson's book, Kidnapped. She found them in a staircase on a wall, walking our way backward through the past. Was that gun in that glass case the gun that did the deed? Was Alan Breck Stewart really the assassin or had he been framed by the conniving and conspiratorial British? Who had plotted to steal from whom? She has vehemently defended his honor and innocence for the 43 years I've known her, and if I want to rile her, vex her and stir her up that's all I have to do, mention Alan Breck Stewart and accuse him of murder – not even accuse him, just suggest it. She descended from Stewarts, but her direct ancestors were here in America before the French-Indian War. The Appin Murder and the French-Indian War were both around 1752. Still, he might have been a cousin.

Bring it up, she gets livid.

Apoplexy is one of our favorite family words.

I enjoy her fits of exasperation. I tease her by stealing and hiding her pillows, occasionally picking up her phone and moving it and hiding it, little pranks like those. No jump scares, never, and no boy who cried wolf. Nope, she might hit me if I did. Trust me, I know.

We rode The Jacobite Steam Train from Fort William to Mallaig, and that was a thrill, really. It is now the Harry Potter train because it was used over the viaduct to film Chamber of Secrets. Karen made video recordings to capture the chugga chugga sound of the steam engine.

There were places we could barely bring ourselves to leave. Tobermory was one of those.

We've had some special places. Orkney Springs, Virginia. Papua New Guinea. We cried and cried, both of us, when we left Papua New Guinea. People must have really wondered about us in Hawaii. "Why is that young couple crying so hard in Honolulu? They must have been scared by the hurricane."

We didn't cry in Scotland.

We didn't cry when we left it.

We were sometimes scared out of our wits driving.

She sang the Huntingtower song over and over.

She doesn't like my version of it, but I change the words a bit to help it make sense. She is certain that others will protest. Let them. But who says "gang" for "going", and "awah" when they mean "away"? No one talks like that anymore. It's a song that should make sense. It makes a lot of sense when you get it, even without the tune. I still have to say "bairnies" instead of "babies", but isn't "bairns" a cool Scottish word, anyway? The Huntingtower song... that's not really its name, it's really "The Duke of Athol" or some such like that. It's a pretty song, a gentle song.

"When you going away, Jamie? Far across the sea, laddie?" it begins.

She loves that song. She's deeply moved by it. I'm deeply moved to hear her sing it.

Huntingtower is like Leonard's Leap in Damsel in Distress – a high born daughter jumped from one tower to another so that her mother would not catch her with her commoner lover. Karen was so pleased and tickled when she found that story in the tourist book from the castle souvenir shop.

We walked all around it and could barely bring ourselves to leave.

To leave a love for Scotland? You cannot leave it, it travels with you.

We named our second daughter Anna Lara, partly because we wanted to sing the Scottish folk song about Annie Laurie. It's a beautiful name. Anna Lara likes for me to say and spell it "Annie Larie" as a pet name, instead of calling her Annie Laurie like the song. Once, in a restaurant in Virginia, a girl stopped to admire baby Annie Larie in her carrier seat and when she heard us say her name the girl turned to her mother and said, "Mom, did you hear? That beautiful baby has a beautiful name, mom. Anna Lara, they named her Anna Lara."

Our firstborn was Sarah Lambert. Princess of the Shining Land. Lambert is a French name that traveled through Scotland.

Kathryn Lynn was our fourth... and Lynn is a pool at a waterfall...

"When you going away, Jamie? Far across the sea, laddie?" the song starts.

"I'll send you a braw new gown, Jennie, I'll send you a braw new gown, lassie," Jamie answers.

That's no gift at all, Jamie. That's no gift at all, laddie. There's no gown in all the world that I want when you're away, Jamie.

Go back to your wife and home, Jamie. Go back to your bairnies three, laddie. And I pray that they never may feel a broken heart like mine, laddie.

Dry that tearful eye, Jennie. My story is all a lie, lassie, for I have no wife or bairnies three and I will wed but thee, lassie.

Think well before you rue, laddie. Think well for fear you rue, Jamie, for I have neither goods nor lands to be a match for you, laddie.

Blair in Athol's mine, Jennie. Little Dunkeld is mine, lassie. St. Johnston's Bower and Huntingtower, and all that is mine is thine, lady.

That woman, Karen, has stuck with me wherever I have gone and kept her eye and heart on me no matter what I have had or lacked, no matter how far I've traveled. In the dark of night, through snowstorm and blizzard, stuck by me through illness and death, endured childbirth and moving.

Blair in Athol is mine, Jennie. Little Dunkeld is mine, lassie. St. Johnston's Bower and Huntingtower, and all that's mine is thine, lady.

And all that is mine is thine lady.

Chapter Four

"I have to talk to you about my thoughts about a conversation I had with some of the men in the church offices about religion," Karen said. "The men in charge are all frustrated because so many churches have troubles. Why are there so many schisms and divisions? They want to fix them and they don't know how. One said maybe we need to focus more on loving Jesus. But I say it's about intention, we have to be intentional and focus our attention on God and then we'd participate with him, and plenty of other good things would come from it. Increase the awareness and understanding of grace and other things will abound."

We were in the kitchen, but I was on my way out, thinking of something I had meant to do and hoping I wouldn't forget it before I got there. But I could see in her face that she didn't want to be put off or be interrupted, so I stopped and waited, knowing I was about to hear an opinion and maybe have to offer up my own, or give some knowledge or insight I had on the topic. She wanted it, she wanted to know my thoughts, and she wanted to tell me her full appraisal of what the church officers were saying.

She went through it a couple more times before she asked me what I thought.

"You can't fix religion," I said. "Religion is *about* fixing, it's always about cleaning up. That's what Jesus said when he criticized the Pharisees. 'You're always cleaning up', and that's what it is. That's what that verse about 'filthy rags' means. 'All your works are filthy rags' is not about *your* works, your works are good and fine, it's about religion being a constant clean up, and then the dirty rags are left to show for it and *they* have to be cleaned and the whole clean up starts over and goes on and on.

"And saying 'let's love Jesus better' doesn't cut it, because what we need to do instead of clean-up is turn to knowing God. Who is he? What does he want? Remember, I used to ask churches at some point every time I preached, 'Where is Jesus right now and what is he doing?' and they couldn't answer."

"That's what I've been saying," Karen said. "It's about intention, we have to be intentional and focus our attention on God and then good things come from that. That's what George and Barbara used to say. If we got to know God then we'd know where Jesus is and what he is doing and we'd participate with him, and plenty of other good things would come from it."

I asked her what is different about how we talk to the kids.

"They get 'How Things Work', how things actually work, and to discern it and think about it, going through life with their eyes open. So they think about things and analyze them."

For most of her life she's had to have The Last Word. She just has to. She has to get it all out and it frustrates her if she can't.

Sometimes I ask, "Please tell me the point first then tell me the rest."

She can add so much detail, and insert so many digressions, and sometimes build up a case like "why we are here" or "why this is important" or "why I am talking about this", and I know I frustrate her because I'll say "spare me the case" or "cut to the chase" or "skip the explanation" when the explanation is as important to her as the point is and maybe has the kernel of the topic that she really needs to think through. Maybe the extra information is really the meat of the topic more so than the point.

People used to tell us we talked to each other too much. A church in Los Angeles told us that men and women just don't talk to each other so much, it doesn't look right.

"You and Karen are always sitting together somewhere with your heads leaning toward each other and you're talking. Stop it."

We didn't stop it.

I asked her what she cares about in talking.

"I want to keep it real. Be forthcoming. We always talked to the kids like they were adults, partners in everything, part of the team, we told them what was what and how things were going."

"What about authenticity?" I asked.

She grimaced.

"I don't like that word, it's overused."

But we talk about authenticity all the time in Art. I even have a lesson I've built on it. Maybe I should show her the PowerPoint for that.

"Do you want things to be authentic?"

"I'm not going to think about authenticity. If it's real then it's authentic. Let's just talk things through and cut the crap and we'll have what's authentic."

What about "genuine"? Do things people talk about need to be genuine?

She winced.

"Don't use that word, either. Ugh, good grief."

I asked her if it's emotionally moving to be known, to realize that someone understands you. Some people will cry when they realize that someone really understands them, that "they get it", and that they are known.

"When does that happen?" she said and arched an eyebrow high.

That prompted several minutes of a long clarifying explanation. I sat and listened.

"Does that make any sense?" she asked when she was done.

"Yes," I replied.

Many times over the years, Karen would say, "You know me. You know things about me no one else would believe."

I don't always know her way of thinking, and she tells me that. I have had to ask her on more than one occasion how she remembers things, how she stores and retrieves her memory, what she sees when she does that, and how she processes. It is all markedly different from mine, and from many other people. Each has their own way, and she has hers.

She has to process through talking. It doesn't matter how long the day is, how exhausted my processing has become, or how much work there has been, or even what hour it is, she still has to talk. Forget "routine", let's go somewhere and talk. "Can we go somewhere and talk?" Even if it just means getting in the car and driving around the neighborhood, can we get away and talk?

Can we talk?

Can we talk with purpose?

Purpose and intentionality, like you know where you're going, like you know the plans that you've made, like you are aware of what's around you and you know the road where you are going.

Karen likes to hear and read well-researched things.

"Those 'Food and where to find it' things just don't interest me at all. I just can't stand hearing people who don't think, who are just parroting what they hear around them."

Doesn't suffer fools lightly? "No, I'm not like that. I just like an exchange of ideas, some give and take, I like a mutual exchange with all sorts of people. It's not that I like to listen. I don't want to just listen, I want to think."

I asked Karen what she sees when she talks and what is in her mind as she speaks and listens takes over her vision. Her memories and the topic at hand are like hanging folders or panels that stretch and unwind not like curtains but like an array of presentations. She can stop them, pull from them and examine them. She often says "pull from them" as in, "You can pull something from that subject," and I wonder if that is what she is thinking and seeing.

She worked on case presentations when she pursued her MBA at James Madison University.

"I have done a lot of presentations on 'Risk Management'. What that means to most folks in business is that you buy insurance, but for me it means that you have to make plans for the worst case scenario so that you don't end up with the worst possible outcome. You want to do better than survive it, you want to come through. You make contingency plans.

"When I ran the summer music festival I used to ask what would happen if we lost all the lawn seating. What if it rained all summer? Could we still make it? Could we make it without the majority of the audience and those ticket sales? And what would be the plan for how to handle that? And I would ask that months before we even needed to think about it, perhaps even right after the last concert of the season, thinking about the next year."

If you're looking for Pygmalion go somewhere else.

How do you relax if you can't process through talking? Are you a fan of anything? How do you unwind?

Karen is the greatest audience. She is the best fan. She gives it rapt attention. She cheers in all the right places. She laughs out loud in all the right places. She wants to talk about it afterward.

And she wants to analyze and talk through everything.

British baking. Iceland. Cave paintings. She went out of her way and missed out on Aberfeldy to visit the Scottish Crannog Centre because she had studied so much about it.

"Have you seen Julianne's Instagram post?" Have you looked at Sarah Lambert's painting? Did you watch the video Anna Lara posted of the baby? Have you read Nathan's latest chapter? He's almost done writing. Did you see the socks that Katy Lynn knitted? The pink is all gone from Adrienne's hair and now it's a frosty blonde, do you like how it's cut? I do.

Karen is the biggest fan.

And she wants to talk.

"Sarah Lambert's going to call at three. I'll go upstairs." And she emerges three hours later.

Six a.m. the phone rings. "It's Anna Lara. Hi, Anna Lara. What is the baby doing? You went where? Tigers? You saw tigers! Oh, cool!"

Nathan sends Karen a manuscript and then wants a critique.

"Okay, Nathan, I liked it, but why did the character do that? I had pictured him another way and I just never expected him to do that."

"Nathan, what is this? Seriously? That's a weird phrase!" And he'll just change it right there. "What do you mean he put the bottle on the table? Where'd we even see him pick it up?" And Nathan will right away take the laptop or the keyboard and make the change and Karen would go right back to reading.

"I love to hear their insights -- from the kids," she says "What they are studying about or reading about or hearing and what they think about it all. I want to know what they are thinking."

In 1992 she surprised me with The World's Greatest Birthday Present, fly fishing lessons and a guided trout fishing trip in Virginia. If I needed rod, line, a reel, and flies, "Buy them," she said. I'm sure that broke the bank. She let me carry Sarah Lambert along when I went fishing, often on my back out into the river.

In 2007 she surprised Anna Lara and Nathan with tickets to see Mandy Patinkin in concert in Wichita. Nathan said, "I have the best family!"

"You have the greatest mother," I said.

When she was with ShenanArts in Staunton, Virginia, we went to see The Tannahill Weavers at the limestone quarry, Lime Kiln, in Lexington. When she was Director of the Shenandoah Valley Music Festival we saw outdoor concerts in the summer at Orkney Springs.

One year she asked me what I would pick for a guest pianist to play with the Fairfax Symphony Orchestra and I said,

74

"Gershwin's Concerto in F," and that's what he played! He was thrilled and pleased by the request! I was so proud.

She played Chopin's Ballade no. 1 in g minor and there hasn't been a day of my life that I have not heard her playing it in my head. I used to daydream that someday I would buy her a studio grand piano, black with ebony and ivory keys, perhaps a Steinway. She insists on keeping the big old upright piano, the family heirloom, and getting replacement strings and having it tuned, and there are plenty of stories that could be told about moving that piano and having it tuned, including the time it nearly crushed me, but who wants to read about all that?

We may have met because I was taking piano lessons and that put me into the Fine Arts Building at the college on the afternoon of a late summer day when she walked in looking for a piano and a practice room.

I used to write poems a bit and so did she. We'd share our own poetry and talk about our literary favorites.

When we met, the college had a nice library. We found a copy of The Knave of Hearts illustrated by Maxfield Parrish. We tried to find his house on our honeymoon.

Jackson, Mississippi, where we met, had a vast Municipal Library and we'd spend hours there and come away with armloads of books. When we lived in small towns, on small jobs and small budgets, the local libraries were the centers of our lives.

But when we first started talking we talked about poetry. Poetry was often the pretense for a visit before we were dating. I'd bring my folders of poems and the literary magazines in which I'd published and Karen would bring out her notebooks and literary magazines and we would share our verses. Then we combed through Norton's anthology and some of Karen's books, and we would recite whatever poems we had memorized. I had collected records of T.S. Eliot reading his poems – how slowly and laboriously could he recite "The Hollow Men" and "The Love Song of J Alfred Prufrock"! But that was the stuff for us. Words, Verses. Meter. The rhymes and rhythms of poetry. The rhythm of longing in the sea.

That's how John Donne's "The Relic" became a favorite. I had to memorize poetry for some of my teachers in middle school and high school, and it became a habit – a very worthwhile habit because it was about the only way I could pass one professor's classes, to have every line committed to memory.

"When my grave is broken up again," begins The Relic.

It's quite macabre, isn't it? Morbid. How could a writer of seduction poetry be so morbid? Famously converted to Christianity, and famous for equivocating Christian conversion with true love, such a device might be a conceit that alluded to The Resurrection of the Dead, and in this case it is a kind of preview of the great resurrection, a way for two dead lovers to bridge the ages and meet again, as if this revelation is an augury or a reminder of The Real Second Coming. You could call it The Second Advent of Two Lovers through a relic, a religious object, in this case a lock of red hair. It is captivating once you think about it.

And we'd think about it, and talk about it, and memorize it, and maybe write our own.

I visited John Donne's effigy each time I went to London.

The Relic, one of our favorites. It begins, "When my grave is

broke up again,

Some second guest to entertain," and then he introduces the relic

of the title,

"And he that digs it spies

A bracelet of bright hair about the bone,

Will he not let us alone and think that there a loving couple lies..."

So, the grave is his grave and the bones are his bones, and

he tied a lock of her red hair around his wrist so that he would be

buried with it and long after his death and decay – after both of

them have gone, she would have to come back again and she

would have to visit his grave in The Resurrection and reclaim her

hair. And that way he would see her again.

More than thirty years after college, when I was trying to

think of a birthday present for Karen, I made a bracelet of gold wire and red floss braided together to recreate the relic of that poem for her, a memento of undying love that could overcome death.

The poem ends with a line we often quote, "And now, alas,

All measure and all language I should pass,

Should I tell what a miracle she was."

A miracle she was... and a miracle she is. She was, and she is.

Chapter Five

A Wedding in India

One song, I have but one song... and it could get repetitious...

We were planning our second daughter's second wedding and the first one which hadn't happened yet was months away.

The first one would be in India, at an auspicious time in mid-January, and the second one would follow in the United States soon after. So we were looking for a wedding venue. How do you rent a wedding venue in ultra-expensive Atlanta when you can barely pay the monthly rent on your house? That's a problem. We live out in "the county" beyond "Greater Atlanta" in suburbia (if there is some version of suburbia beyond exurb and suburb and exists over the next hill and beyond the horizon past the inner loop and the outer loop and up the extension) and even here in this

80

town there wasn't a venue we could afford. So we searched. She searched. And she found it. She is a very determined girl.

I have a motto which I often say, "Whatever I lack, I will make up for in determination."

That young woman beats me.

It had brought us to Nash Farm, nearly an hour's drive from home. And I was standing there realizing that it was a battlefield between a Confederate museum and the barn-like building where we were going to conduct a wedding. And I realized that I was staring at a black obelisk that was a Confederate memorial, and on it was my great grandfather's cavalry company, and my great grandfather had been there with his brother-in-law. Then I realized that I had read about that battle, Lovejoy Station, but I didn't pay attention or take it in. And that was the place where we were going to have our daughter's international wedding.

Maybe if there is a War of the Sexes it's going on around us but we aren't in it, but maybe others want to pull us into it but let's not let them.

Have you ever noticed people in the park just sitting in some spot unaware of the vast park in the enormous city in the great wide world in the incomprehensibly vast universe, and there they are occupying the smallest piece of real estate there is but while they're sitting there on the grass or in their corner on the floor of the mall they own it, and they don't care.

We are grandparents in India. I say it all the time, "Our India family", "our family in India"...

But my toes were at a memorial to a battle in the Civil War which I only recognized and connected with because I had spent the past five years searching for records of our ancestry and I had blindly and unknowingly walked right up to a shiny polished stone stele that said, in effect that my great grandfather and my great grandmother's brother had been there defending that ground in a battle.

The two prospective newlyweds met at an Ivy League college, one of the oldest in the country, the University of Pennsylvania, in Philadelphia, twelve to fourteen hours of interstate driving away from our home.

We had agreed that the first wedding would be in India. The auspicious day was in mid-January. The likelihood of snow in Atlanta in February or March is small so we planned the second ceremony for February or March, to be convenient for the couple who would be completing their honeymoon travel and could swing through America to get married again. That way all the family and friends here in these United States could be satisfied that we had a Christian wedding amid the traditions of our community and families. We couldn't find a pastor to consecrate the wedding because they each and all wanted to have some counseling time with the couple, and when they said counseling time they meant days and weeks and possibly a commitment of months, so we weren't going to do that. We couldn't, we just didn't have that kind of time and availability. Consequently it fell to me then to conduct the wedding, and to be wedding planner and wedding coach.

If you want to experience colossal "sticker shock" price a wedding cake within a hundred miles of Atlanta. We had only moved from Kansas a few years earlier. We still drove the used car that we drove when we moved from Kansas. So Anna Lara, who loves baking (wow, oh boy, that would be another story) talked to her mother, and Karen came up with a homemade layer cake recipe and Karen made the tower and Anna Lara made the icing and decorated it herself. It was a fantastic cake, the best. We should probably at this moment be running a bakery of nothing but wedding cakes with that recipe at Atlanta prices. Karen considers it one of her great victories.

Our first daughter's wedding was in Kansas and it was a brilliantly self-done job in a rental tea castle in one of the larger cities in the northeastern corner of Kansas. Aunts and uncles catered the foods and desserts. It was brilliant and beautiful. It was fifteen hundred miles away on the far end of a two-day drive through Tennessee, Kentucky, Indiana, and Missouri, beyond the Lewis-and-Clark arch, across the wide Missouri. Sarah Lambert and Jordan met in middle school and had been friends through high school.

Midwestern accents don't sound the same as southern ones, you know. They're different and some of the vowels are flat. After living her childhood in Kansas, Julianne the fifth child says "our" as if it was "are". It's kind of like "pee-can" or "puh-con". All different slices of a pie...

The proudest and happiest parents and siblings, and former neighbors were at that wedding. It was beautiful. Some weddings are such wonderful experiences that you'd just like to stay there, hour after hour, day after day and live in them.

The groom and his brothers. Their families. Their friends. It really was a fine wedding.

For the wedding in Georgia, Anna Lara's second wedding in two months, we were trying to reckon how to string the lights in the big empty rental hall, just how to make an arbor or arch to set a stage that would look special and memorable for the wedding at Nash Farm. Anna Lara wanted to hang the lights from a Conestoga wagon wheel. She even found a rusty one at an antique mall and we bought it. I think it was really the rim of an old tractor wheel. She wanted to pull it up by a rope and pulley and have it hang over the guests like a rustic chandelier, and from it strings of lights would radiate to the walls like stars in the summer sky above Kansas. But I thought it was too heavy and there was no way to balance it and keep it level. It worried me, so I made a wooden frame in substitute.

To prepare for the wedding in India, to get us ready for the culture before traveling, we watched a few Indian movies. It probably would have worked better if I had watched a Cecil B. DeMille production or two, like The Greatest Show on Earth or The Ten Commandments because those were what I thought of when I walked into the wedding tent. Nothing prepared us for the size of that tent, or the numbers of guests.

Huge. Red. Colossal. Spectacular. In there, off to the side was an intimate space defined by cushions and curtains to set it apart from the food bars and liquor bars and buffets and the stage with two luxurious chairs like thrones, and there in that intimate little space, like a booth at a major league stadium, was where we joined hands and had the wedding.

Vashisht, the groom, leaned to me and in his characteristic calm and gentle wise way said, "Whatever they are saying, you think of your God and what you believe." Very thoughtful.

Words like Kaballah and the Hindu red kavala bracelet seem too similar to not be related. Many of the things in a Hindu wedding seemed familiarly like a Jewish wedding. I had no problem with questions about faithfulness, duty and devotion.

It seemed to me, as best as I could understand the words and deeds of the service, was that they were asking Vashisht a lot of questions about whether he would be dutiful and faithful and whether he would take care of Anna Lara. Would he define his life as being devoted to meeting her needs? I liked that, and I preached the same sermon in Georgia at Nash Farm, saying similar things like, "The best way to take care of ourselves is to take care of our spouse." What if the whole reason for my existence is to be here for Karen and to meet her needs?

Every semester I teach about Jan van Eyck's Arnolfini Wedding. I have seen it twice in The National Gallery in London. What I tell my students as I stand in front of a projection of a jpeg of that oil painting is that in the 1400's they really didn't have to go through all that. You can take a course in medieval courtship and marriage and you can read Romeo and Juliet and you will find out that the pains of Romantic courtship and the pilgrimage to Cythera and courtly love had not taken over Europe in the 1400's. All you had to do to get married in medieval Europe in 1400 was hold hands and say "yes" and maybe pledge an oath and maybe, if you were determined to do it and go to all that trouble you might go to the church which in those days was also the courthouse and write your names and record your wedding with witnesses and post the bans. You didn't have to hire The Single Greatest and Most

Respected and Widely Known Oil Painter in the Netherlands and stand around in heavy expensive clothes for over a hundred hours during the course of two or three weeks. The symbolism in that painting says everything Karen and I were trying to say with our wedding. A worship service with God as witness. People asked us, "Why did you have everyone sing four hymns at your wedding? Four! Hymns! With a choir!" It was a worship service about the Bridegroom of all bridegrooms and His bride, how He searched for her and found her. It was about His victory.

Vashisht rode high above the crowd in raiments fit for a prince. He was the victor, arriving in victory after hours and miles of crowds – especially his friends! – harassing him and taunting him and tricking him and trying to hold him back. It even involved stealing, buying and ransoming shoes and redeeming them by buying them back. The victor had come for his bride. He was determined to get through.

The prince had come into his kingdom. His father spoke to him that way. "Now you are a man, my son. At last my boy has become a man."

We tie bracelets of bright floss around our wrists and we make promises and we remember and we hope to God that He remembers His promises. As reminder to himself He can look at the red blood on His own wrists.

Sarah Lambert and Jordan had to get remarried only a year after their Kansas wedding because they couldn't find their marriage license. They were living in Asheville and they had to go to Gatlinburg in a hurry to get another marriage license, which also meant a quickie Gatlinburg wedding. You may be picturing that quaint kitschy chapel in tourist town but this one took place at a hardware store. The upside was that they found an English pub there on the same road. It's the greatest little pub and introduced me to Smithwick's, an ale that has only been in production since the 1700's.

We have had four weddings and only two daughters of our five have gotten married, and each of those two had to get married twice to the same young men. Apart from the charm of the hardware store, there wasn't as much decoration at Jordan and Sarah Lambert's second event.

As the wise man said, this saying requires patience. If I'm not mistaken, the Apostle Paul said that too, and so did Chuang Tzu and Lao Tze and Miyamoto Musashi.

You know, you can only be Classical and live in self-satisfaction in your Western Civilization Greek world if you ignore and discount everything else. Either Western Civilization is totally right and you're right and everyone else is wrong and everything else is mistaken or you have to admit that you may have missed something. You can accept that Trojan horse but it will get you. One night they'll come out of that horse and steal your shoes and your chickens.

One song, I have but one song... there is a bridegroom coming and he wants his bride and he wants his shoes and he already has the victory.

Chapter Six

Karen introduced me to Richard Halliburton's posthumous book, The Book of Marvels, a collection of his adventures and photographs of distant and exotic places. Pictures were called "book plates". I think she had it with her at college.

There were tales of sneaking into Mecca during the Hajj, traveling down the Panama Canal without a ship at the world's smallest historic toll of thirty-five cents, and visiting the Roman amphitheater and colonnaded arcade at Palmyra in Syria. It was good accompaniment to imagining T.E. Lawrence in Arabia and Howard Carter and Lord Carnarvon in Egypt and Sir Richard Burton's exploration of the Nile and the search for the source. Those were the kinds of things that took us to the library together.

How had a man from Tennessee disguised himself well enough to join the Hajj?

The world of maps and pictures was as intriguing as the world itself, like a separate and parallel reality, the world of travel and adventure.

Karen had been to Rome and Venice. Her family lived half a year in Alaska after traveling the Alaska Highway, a journey by car through Canada. The road, she said, was like a terrible washboard, bump, bump, bump, jostling and jaggedly jiggling, clacking your teeth with every mile over hundreds of miles. They had broken an axle but they carried a spare. Who carries a spare axle? That was amazing.

She had wandered among The Mountains of the Moon.

Well, no, those are in Africa... She had walked through The Craters of the Moon National Park in Idaho, and tiptoed on the tops of rocks and buttes and places west. She'd visited Mammoth Cave, the long walk in the dark, and eaten in a café amid stalagmites under stalactites on a journey to the center of the earth. She had ridden horseback up Mount LeConte. Subsequently we've done some of those things, the same trips her parents took their four

94

children on. Some places we have taken our children along, and some places we have gone to by ourselves. The two of us had to walk up Mount LeConte because they no longer do the horse tours and we didn't eat in Mammoth Cave because they closed the café in the middle of that great long walk in the dirt and dark.

I used to joke, before I met Karen and maybe even to her after we met, that my travels included Pelahatchie Lake and Duck Hill, Mississippi, but I had actually spent a year in military school near The Ruins of Windsor and I had been to New Orleans several times, and Memphis while my sister lived there, and I would occasionally drive to Natchez and Vicksburg just to dine. In those days that seemed extravagant.

Karen had her books – The Black Arrow, Raggedy Ann and Andy – and her photographs – a sepia tone of her grandmother that she felt resembled her – and her cherished objects, like "Big Granny's Stick" and General Beauregard's tea set. I don't recall her having any cherished affectionate objects like a teddy bear or a special pillow. She was good at needlepoint – her first job after college was selling embroidery floss at a needlepoint shop in Fondren.

She was a fount of memories. Following behind her brother, Steve, scouting through the woods sounded like The Adventures of Tom Sawyer. She snuck a ride to Jackson once, as a preschooler, hiding beneath blankets on the floorboard of the back seat, and nearly scared her mother, who was at home in Hattiesburg frantically searching for her, half to death.

"Don't you wish Karen was along?" Dr. Harris asked her brother Steve.

"Oh, yes, I do," answered Steve, and she sprang up in back and said, "I am along! You don't have to miss me, I'm here!"

Karen has stories and memories and tales to tell, family stories and ghost stories, and she will sing long forgotten songs that Granny sang to her, like the two children in the railroad car with their mother in a coffin in the train car in back.

She doesn't have "a memory palace". In her mind time and memories are images like files and folders in Windows that stretch out and spring back accordion style. She can reach for one and expand it and explore it, savor it vividly, then move to another one. The expandable files and hanging displays of Karen's mind. They hang like curtains or perhaps like drops, not backdrops per se, not precisely like curtains but easily accessible and searchable.

She doesn't use mnemonic devices like I do, like remembering the 10, 2 and 4 on a Dr. Pepper bottle to remember a clock face and the ten and two of fly casting and that fish will often bite at ten, two or four and four is "tea time". She doesn't do that.

She doesn't have a memory palace.

She doesn't hide a memory under an urn in Portmeirion and have to travel there to pick it up and see it. When she explores a place in her mind she enjoys the place and its memories are there, like Market Square and Duke of Gloucester Street. She enjoys the sights and scenery, the decorous occasions, and delights in the maze for the thing itself.

The storage of her memories in her mind isn't a file cabinet or a library with tomes.

Her memories hang like the paintings and artifacts in modern museums, like "the stacks" in the William & Mary library. She can slide them out of the way and pull them back and rifle through them and push them out of the way. Each in its place on a collapsible and expandable timeline.

Ask her and she will tell you very excitedly about what she sees and how she remembers, using the screen on her Kindle or her iPhone to swipe right or swipe left and choose a file and expand it with her fingertips, enlarging a detail in her imagination until it fills a screen. It's not a good idea to ask her about things like this while she is driving or she'll suddenly slow down, decelerating to 25 mph in a 40 mph zone because she is seeing what she is saying, seeing the memory she is talking about.

You can ask her about something and her face will be radiant and confident as if she had an air of command on the deck of a ship. Let's go. We're ready.

For a while there she was reading about Hornblower. That "take charge" comparison is not accidental or casual or misplaced.

Comparisons can lead to long clarifying explanations.

She does not like to be compared to Wendy, even though for years I teasingly said, "I'm hurted, Wendy," and made jibing references to Peter Pan. I wouldn't object to being compared to Peter Pan. I don't think I object to comparisons to much of anything. But she would. She is her woman herself.

When I first met her she quoted Mary Poppins, saying that she was "practically perfect in every way."

We have our sayings.

Some came from Patrick McGoohan and The Prisoner. "Questions are a burden for others. Answers are a prison for oneself." Which we of course mean sarcastically.

"Living well is the best revenge," has been attributed to George Herbert, but his vast list of proverbs may have been gathered from others. I always thought that saying came from F. Scott Fitzgerald.

Yep, we're like living reference libraries of quotations.

The world is full of places to go to, and so is the mind.

She became intrigued by how her children think. Who has a spatial memory, like an engineer or an artist? Nathan drew a dragon on a slip of paper and the folds of the dragon like the folds of the paper required a four dimensional understanding of time and space – and he was in second grade. Who is verbal? Who is nonverbal? How do they process? What kind of speed do they have, or extra time do they need?

An MBA, she considered going back to school for a Masters in psychology or educational psychology because she understands testing and the ways of the brain.

I am not going to list facts about my experience as an educator, I am just going to humbly say that she explained testing and research to me, and has to frequently remind me of the names of the tests and what can be known from them and which child has had which tests and what was ascertained through those tests. She says, "What can be pulled from them."

The labyrinth of the mind requires a ball of string and she is Theseus and Ariadne, both, with a string of glittering jewels, in command enough to not care a fig about the minotaur or worry about slaying him or whether or not he is just bones, like the calcified cave bears of Chauvet.

They are all curiosities. Curiosities in a menagerie of memories and explorations, and the mechanical puzzles of spinning machines in the music room of the palace of the mind.

A museum is a wonderful thing, except of course a museum of ship models in Mystic Seaport on your honeymoon when you're tired and hungry.

"I'm tired and I'm hungry; can we go eat?"

"But I've all my life wanted to see these," I said, as I kept moving from glass exhibit case to glass exhibit case, through gallery after gallery, up floor after floor, staring at models of sailing vessels and trying to guess at the light settings for my Argus C4.

"But I'm tired and I'm hungry. Aren't you tired and hungry? I'm tired and I'm hungry."

She kept saying it. I kept ignoring her. I went right on examining the ship models.

So she punched me. In the kidney. In a public museum. On our honeymoon. I learned my lesson.

This is how you learn empathy and to care about the needs of others.

No such incidents have taken place since, in the exhibit halls of museums, some with their high arches like the ribs of a bleached whale, some with mezzanines overlooking the skeletons of mastodons, the pachyderms, the panoplies, and thick glass windows to swimming creatures that would be more at home in the sea. In the cities, in the countryside, along the highways and hedges of the world, we have walked through castles and cathedrals and museums. The file folders and cases and hanging displays of the memory of the universe.

In Scotland, Karen was interested in how the geology of the British Isles had formed and what that explained about the geography of its different regions and our journeys.

When we were two newlyweds and missionaries in Papua New Guinea the islands now known as Vanuatu were called New Hebrides. I thought about that when we went to the West Hebrides of Scotland. Vanuatu and Papua New Guinea, some of the shakiest and quakiest places in the world. We loaded airplanes and ran a guest house (briefly) in Lae during a 120 degree Fahrenheit Christmas. I swear that it was so hot that the plastic tree wilted. I could prove it, too; I have a picture.

We drove an hour from our home in Georgia – maybe an hour and a half – to visit the Etowah Indian Mounds. She wanted to see everything. Every worn step up the mound and every trampled path was important, every detail of the fragments of fabrics, every carving, and every beaten copper plate was intriguing, just as intriguing as Vindolanda and Housesteads along Hadrian's Wall. How did these people live? Did they dance? And what did they dance to? What was their music like?

The memory of humankind stretches out like a scroll or a spring and waves or coils and she pulls it and she pushes it and she colors a new place on a new map. Look, here's the map of Edinburgh in 1870. You can find Greyfriars on the map. And there's the street where we stayed. Look, see how close we were to John Knox's House? And this is the spot where St. Columba set foot when he landed on Iona, and that box we saw in the museum in Edinburgh, that looked like the chapel where they put his ashes. Maybe it was the relic that contained his ashes, or at least some of them. Did you see the headless horseman on the map of Mull? I'm sorry we missed that. I wish I'd seen that map first, before we drove to the ferry for Iona. And the Cloisters, here in New York, this was made of parts of churches and abbeys and monasteries they rescued from Europe and pieced together here.

She has always been like this. Maybe I have, too.

"Edgar Allen Poe's house isn't far from here, let's go there."

"They give tours at Carter's Grove Plantation, let's go out there and see."

"Look down, they found the foundation from the House of Burgesses at Jamestowne. My ancestor, Robert Wynne was Speaker of the House of Burgesses in the sixteen hundreds."

Do the seashells want to go back to the sea? Is there a blood that knows its own?

She heard an owl. Listen. There must be owls in the neighborhood.

She saw a hawk. "That's my spirit animal."

What does it take to be fully a person? Is a human being like "a little world made cunningly"? Can you draw maps of a human being? Well, obviously, we've all seen them, the circulatory system and the digestive system and the skeleton and the musculature. We watched Jonathan Miller and The Body in Question when it aired. Now they wonder if the lymph system may have command of health as actively as the nervous system. Do the interstitial fluids transmit information and make commands?

For years she was terrified of cancer. Her mother had breast cancer. Her mother died of liver cancer when Karen was 19 and in college. Karen struggled with Gartner duct cysts until after the third child was born, fourteen years into our marriage. I don't know when the shadow of fear left her face, when something like panic stopped circulating in her eyes. I just know that it's gone. She seems less cautious and wary than she did when I first met her, when she would lean uncertainly against a wall or a door frame and silently watch me, not so sure that I could be trusted.

The topic of death may have vanished one funeral home at a time or one delivery room at a time as our choir director died while I held the handles of his wheelchair, when her mother died, when my father died while we were in New Guinea, when her father and my mother died two months apart and we made long journeys with carloads of kids who learned to play and entertain themselves at funeral homes. All of our children were born happy and healthy one after another through 16 years of childbearing and childbirth. Life and death, joy and grief, in successive years, along paths and byways in cities and counties and states and countries in year after progressive year. A pilgrimage. At some point you embrace being a survivor.

"I won, I'm living."

He's not the best character to quote, Aged Pistol in Henry V, but he had a point when he said, "But, lambkins, we live."

Let us follow the trail and see where it goes in the confidence that it must go somewhere.

Or, we can study the books and maps, like we did for weeks before we went to Hong Kong.

I did not know anything when we went to Papua New Guinea. I didn't even grasp the general geography of Los Angeles before we went there first, before traveling to New Guinea. In 1980 I generally understood east and central Texas, but it was at least a decade later before I could accurately place Corpus Christi,

Galveston and Port Arthur. I really came to understand where Wichita Falls is and what their weather is like only after moving to Kansas and following the tracks of tornadoes, and it was during that time that I finally came to appreciate The Panhandle and where Amarillo really is, and where the Rio Grande flows to the Gulf of Mexico. Spend long enough in a place, like nine years in Kansas, and you come to know it better, especially if you jump in the car and go everywhere. Then you come to live in maps.

We came to know and love a number of places out west. Old forts where our motto became "Lest We Forget". Old trails like the Santa Fe Trail and the Chisholm Trail, both of which we lived along. And we visited the stops that began the Pony Express.

One of her favorite movies is Rio Grande. It is like the nexus of too many travels, too many moves. The first trumpet sounds and we stop and listen to the opening score and our hearts melt. Victor Young's music is just incredible and evocative. I've already talked about folks songs, there are other old songs. We had a CD of Songs of the Seventh Cavalry that we played in the car when we traveled in Kansas to Fort Larned, and to see the fossil fish with another fossil fish inside it at the Sternberg Museum in Fort Hays. Is there a more rousing tune than "The Girl I Left Behind Me"?

"I'm lonesome since I crossed the hill,

And o'er the moorlands sedgy,

Such heavy thoughts my heart do fill,

Since parting from my Sally.

I seek no more the fine and gay,

For each just does remind me

How sweet the hours I passed away

With the girl I left behind me."

And we used to whistle The Gary Owen until it got stuck forever in our first daughter's mind.

A picnic in the red blowing dust of Monument Valley is not as charming as you might imagine. Camping in a thunderstorm in

Big Meadows is not so glamorous, either. Waking up to wade from a tent after the rainstorms of the night turned the level campground into a lake is not what we expected at Walt Disney World. And it is monstrous guilt when your three year old collapses from altitude sickness at the Yogi Bear Campground miles up in the Rockies of Colorado.

The tired songs of the old Colorado trails, the weary melodies of the Prairie. Not altogether unlike the sad songs of the boatmen trailing their oars in the lochs of Scotland. Do you reckon the men who drove the Herefords and the Highland cattle took the same songs to the cattle drives of the west? The Poor Luckless Laddie or some such song is the same tune as The Streets of Laredo, isn't it? With much the same words? And so is St. James Infirmary Blues.

Sigh. I don't have the blues, but at the end of a long day I'm weary. I want to go home and greet my angel.

"When I've done my work of day,

And I row my boat away,

On the waters of Loch Tay,

As the evening light is fading,

And I look upon Ben Lowers

Where the after glory glows,

And I think on two bright eyes and the melting mouth below.

She's my beauteous nighean rudh,

My joy and sorrow, too,

And although she is untrue

Well, I cannot live without her.

For my heart's a boat in tow,

And I'd give the world to know

Why she means to let me go

As I sing horee horo."

I cannot live without her.

She is not exactly like Nighean Rudh, whoever that was, nor am I the Loch Tay boat man, although I do like to canoe and kayak, and I took a course in sailing, and I used to rent a Sunfish and sail on the Ross Barnett Reservoir, something I gave up when dating her.

You see, she gets motion sickness.

She hurls from the gunnels of the boat.

The drive through western Virginia to the Maple Festival in McDowell was more than half the family could handle.

We look at maps and if a road has too many switchbacks and hairpin turns we say, uh oh, better not go there.

We have some sayings in our family: "She went too many places. There were too many stops. Oh no there were too many right hand turns."

If I ever wanted to escape, I wouldn't have to spend a night at the YMCA, all I would have to do is step onto a boat and drift away from shore. She would be helpless, unable to follow.

It's not like she can't cross water, she rode the James River ferry from Jamestowne to Scotland, Virginia, and ferries in Scotland from Oban to Craignure on Mull, and from there the ferry from Lochaline to Fishnish and consequently the Corran-Ardgour ferry so we could get to Fort William. And there was a ferry to and from Iona and she was fine on all of them. But she just can't row a boat.

Our oldest daughter said that she and her husband daydream of living in a houseboat. Karen told them, then I'll never be able to visit; so much for that.

It doesn't have to be a boat that makes her lose her cookies, it could happen just watching a virtual tour, like a film or something on YouTube. I learned this when she nearly lost her lunch in the 360 viewing room that they used to have at Walt Disney World. There are videos that she just can't watch.

It's embarrassing to the world adventurer to admit that her stomach is upside down.

Chapter Seven

Karen is frequently concerned about forgiveness. What she's concerned about is whether or not I'm too bitter and harbor too much resentment and whether or not I even get the right idea about forgiving.

Here is one thing I say: to forgive something someone has to die. You have to say, "That ship sailed", "that person left for a far country," that man is dead and gone, I died and that died with me, I took it with me to the grave. And so it's gone and we won't mention it again. Usually the one that has to die is me, or some part of me.

But, then, after that you have to go on living.

A difference between the two of us is that she stores her memories and saves all of them, and not many of them are traumatic. Me, I'm prone to panic attacks and suppressed or repressed memories. Upset me, and whether I want it to or not, my mind erases your name and image where I can't for the life of me recall them and buries things away to freakishly bring them back at the picnic.

I'm not afraid of the cave or the Minotaur or the bones of the dead he leaves behind him, but, damn, do I have to remember a thing that makes me feel bad?

But she worries because Jesus said that if you can't forgive then you won't be forgiven, or something like that. Don't be too legalistic about it, whatever Jesus meant he could not have precisely meant that because it would contradict the gospel and salvation would be impossible.

I don't know why she worries about my blood pressure, I don't think that I get pissed off nearly as much as she does.

She's a wonder when she's angry.

She was attacked once, in Harrisonburg, Virginia, at the car in the parking lot while changing the baby's diaper. The man came up behind her and tried to shove her into the car, and she gritted her teeth and spat out, "Oh, no, you don't!" and bracing her hands against the doorframes pushed him back. But he let go and went away when she resisted. She grabbed up baby Sarah Lambert who through her pacifier said, "Oh, no!", and Karen said, "That's right, oh, no," and stomped back into the public library to announce, "I've been attacked!"

Karen was really angry, but she wished she had seen his face and had a really good look at him, to "look him in the eye". She yelled, "Turn around and look at me!", as he ran off.

"I wish I'd crammed her dirty diaper in his face!"

What followed were the police coming to the library, recounting the incident, looking through pages and pages of photographs, failing to find a matching face, and describing the assailant for a sketch, but no one ever found him.

She had bad bruises on her shins from pushing against the car frame in her anger pushing her attacker away.

She told me about a story from childhood that she doesn't like to tell because it involved someone who it would be better not to reveal because some other people would be upset. As one person we won't name said, "Your father would kill him." The story has a very telling moment, which is that the perpetrator who did some inappropriate touching told her, "Don't tell anyone."

"Don't tell anyone." Nope, that's not right.

My motto is, tell everybody. Go out on the sidewalk and shout. Immediately. Tell as many as you can tell. That isn't always the best advice, but I say start there and have that as advice because the tool of villains and bullies is suppression. Silence the accuser. Silence the witness. "Don't tell anyone." Don't comply with that.

I've twice been offered settlements or buy-outs or severance and in each case part of what they wanted was a guarantee that I would never tell anyone. Ha! I just told you.

This woman cares about forgiveness and relationships and doesn't want people to become distant and uncommunicative.

She used to talk cautiously about men fighting. "It's a serious thing for one man to hit another. Granny says that when a man hits another man it can be deadly. It can lead to serious things."

She worried that a child might become embittered and go away and never talk to parents or siblings again.

"Never let the sun go down upon your wrath, Granny said," quoted Karen.

We weren't going to have huffy arguments. No crossed arms. No running to your room and slamming and locking the door. You can't run home to your parents. Fat lot of good that effort would have been with one parent dead and another committed to an institution, but it's the thought that counts not the practical implications.

When we were kids everyone played with toy guns, and you'd shoot and they'd say, ha!, you missed me, but sometimes you'd have to say you'd been hit – killed or wounded – just to be fair and a good sport and keep the game going. So, you'd count to ten and then come back.

There are times, though, where things have been said that can't be taken back. There are ways of discarding a person that tell them that you thought they were trash all along. There are times when you die and you can't come back.

So, Karen is proactive and tries to keep the wounds and deaths and fights and gaps from happening, to mend the broken spirit before it falls to the ground.

Karen does not have these bitter thoughts.

We are trying to construct here the model of the three-dimensional woman. They had those in the toy stores when we were kids. I think it was actually called The Visible Woman or maybe The Invisible Woman because she was see-through like glass. Clear plastic.

Perhaps this is the four-dimensional woman, existing across time, able to take the timeline and stretch it out or roll it back like an accordion.

Or the five dimensional woman, who like a goddess exists as a seer and The All Mother beyond space and time yet in them, kin to Kronos, but never sleeping.

Perhaps she is like the mother in Revelation 12, cloaked by the sun, with the moon at her feet and a crown of stars, who had to run away to the Prairie – excuse me, I meant The Wilderness, for a time.

Let's not become too grandiose and poetic here, we're talking about someone who gets car sick, who can't be punctual to save her own life – who *won't* be punctual, who refuses to be punctual.

"Don't rush me, I'll be ready."

"But it's 6:30 and we won't make it by 7:00 if we don't leave now."

"I said I'd be ready at 7:00."

"But we can't wait until 7:00 to leave, we're supposed to be there at seven!"

She isn't just not punctual, she defies punctuality.

Defiant, there's another word she hates.

I like the word "defiant".

Defiant.

"Don't say that. I don't like it."

She makes a face.

Defiant, defiant, defiant. See? I said it.

She married me for love not money – I had no money, or property. Seems, uh, pretty defiant to me.

She married me for love not social status, I didn't have that, either. That seems pretty defiant, too.

She married me when every girl in her dorm said don't. We don't think he looks right. We don't like the look in his eyes. And he's an artist – that's the lowest cut of all – what? He might cut off an ear? Maybe he'll cut off one of your ears.

There are a lot of words I like: defiant, indomitable, indefatigable...

There's a chapter coming where I have to admit to some stupid mistakes. Ugh. I hate thinking about them but I have to. The girls – Karen and five daughters – never let me forget them. So, there's forgiveness, I guess, but there isn't forgetting?

Two classical characters I often think about are Sisyphus and Prometheus. If something looks like a Sisyphean task then forget it, I am out of here. But are bad memories like the ravens that gnaw at Prometheus's liver? Ravens are supposed to be symbols of eternal life. Are bad memories and regrets immortal? Will they always come back?

Lest you feel cheated by the denouement, I'll tell you now that my regrets are so small you'd say, "What?" Like a colleague of mine told me recently, "I can tell how authoritarian you are by that smiley face you put in your email." Then he smiled.

Karen needs a sounding board to bounce things off of, she needs an echo. Sometimes she's only empathetic by referral. I let her read a chapter, and her reaction was just sort of eh until two of the girls reacted and then she wanted to talk about it. Sometimes she has to see someone else wear something to know that it's right. She has successfully written many grants, and she needs someone to read them, comment on them. My job is to read things aloud and maybe to wordsmith them.

Partners, we're partners. It's a team.

She has her own ways of reacting to things and they aren't predictable or consistent. I only realized that I was about to be bitten by a copperhead on the trail behind me because she covered her ears and shrieked and quickly walked away.

I felt horrible at the times when she cried, which thankfully have not been often, not only because I caused it but also because her face completely transformed and her chin dropped, and her mouth became a V and it was just terrible and helpless. And I am actually seriously concerned that one day she will get so angry she bites through her lower lip. She has bruised it on occasion.

You don't tickle. Tickling could get you puncture wounds and she would say that you deserve it.

We are friends. Someone to talk to. Someone to share with.

I am not going to lie and make some kind of stupid claim that I would rather die than disappoint her because I have disappointed her plenty. I wouldn't let her down if I could help it but there are times when I just couldn't help it. Her birthday on the first day of classes. Anniversary, yes, but the bank account got emptied by Christmas or that bill we had to pay. I know you want to sit and make plans but my brain is exhausted from midterm testing and grading and credentialing and the five things we also had to engage in with the kids. Decision fatigue. Responsibility fatigue. Resources depleted. Perhaps human beings should add some kind of observable sensors and read-out mechanism with colored lights and such like automobile diagnostics where another person can look at them and say, "Gosh, honey, I see that, it says right here that you are low on coolant and your energy is critically low and needs to recharge." That will, I'm sure, be the next great advancement in smartphones.

If the situation ever actually comes where it's disappoint or die, I'll just have to say, "I have a sanctuary in the hearts of them that love me," and expect to pop off *and* disappoint. It seems guaranteed.

Chapter Eight

Natural Childbirth

Rick told Ilsa that they would always have Paris, but I told Karen that we will always have Hong Kong.

We stopped in Hong Kong on our trip back from Papua New Guinea. The landing was practically vertical in those days – and I mean nose down – onto the world's shortest runway that seemed to start and end at the edge of the water. In my memory I keep thinking we stayed there a week, but on reflection I think we were there for four days.

In Hong Kong we were introduced to Dim Sum and how to really eat with chopsticks and how to eat the local cuisine not the American franchises such as pizza. We traveled to an island on a ferry, past the junks, and we saw the hydrofoils that plied the waters to Macau. We rode the incline, "The Peak Tram", the funicular train of Victoria. Hong Kong was still a Crown Colony then.

I had a leather jacket tailor made in twenty-four hours from a sketch I did in the shop and a paper pattern that the tailor created while I stood there for measurements.

We learned about Kowloon and about Victoria and about the near islands. We stayed in the YMCA, which was located behind The Peninsula Hotel, so it looked like we were staying elegantly as guests of the Peninsula, and we even slipped through the lobby a few times, to see and be seen, as they say, giggling or trying to not giggle as we made our way to the really small and plain room we had at "the Y", but, gee, we were in Kowloon, in Hong Kong, in the shadow of the grand Peninsula Hotel. How cool is that?

Everyone everywhere was dressed so nicely. The best clothes. The best shoes. The streets and sidewalks were clean. There were signs forbidding spitting. Spitting was a crime. Don't Do It!

The really memorable thing was the train up Victoria Peak and getting out to stand on the overlooks. Karen wasn't sure that we should take it, it meant a lot of time in our trip, it might cost too much, she wasn't sure who or what we might encounter at the top and whether or not we would be able to get back down. It turned out that it didn't take long to get there, the cost wasn't much, and our companions seemed to be teenagers and young adults that were laughing and talking.

There was an overlook halfway up and at the top there was the grand overlook that has become iconic of Hong Kong, perhaps of any Asian harbor city.

It became iconic for us. It became one of our most loved trips, and four years later it was still so vivid and precious to us that we used our memories as our focus imagery in Lamaze class in 1987.

Breathe. Blow. Count. Have something to think about.

We expected our first child in December 1987. The due date was the twenty second and that seemed like nice timing before Christmas. We were 900 miles from our old home, not as far as the 9,000 miles to Papua New Guinea, but we felt it, updating family by phone, ordering things for the nursery from the Sears catalog, watching the hot Virginia summer turn to chilly autumn and wondering how to prepare for winter.

If the real definition of courage is being determined to go through with something even when you're afraid, pregnancy and childbirth must be right up there on the stress scale and the courage list.

So that's why we were at Lamaze class, every Tuesday with our pillows, on the floor practicing breathing and counting and focus.

Could you think of things, such as treasured experiences, to share to help with delivery? The whole idea was relaxation and reassurance for natural childbirth.

I was designated as helper or friend or caregiver – I don't remember, I just don't recall the words "man and woman", or "husband and wife", or "parents", or "mother and father", and I do remember being corrected by the instructor once, somewhat briskly, to not say those words but to say "caregiver" or whatever I'd been labeled so I would earnestly concentrate on my role.

Karen wanted me to cooperate. I was cooperating. And to be serious. I was serious. Glibness, smart aleck sarcasm, cleverness, and wittiness are not reassuring and comforting and supportive – and I guess those were unfortunately my specialties back then. Perhaps I looked sarcastic. I mean, how else would I go around with my face? Or maybe I looked like I would run off?

You heard stories of women screaming in the delivery room, begging for pain medicines, pleading for it to end, breaking their husbands' arms or hands, threatening the doctors, cursing, swearing, what have you... What would we be like? Perhaps we seemed too relaxed and not prepared for violence. Casual and unprepared.

Dr. Lamaze is rumored to have rated intelligent women as unfit for natural childbirth. Is that really what he thought? Was he a turnip head? Did he not know that people read and study, research and prepare? How did he become a doctor? In The Middle Ages I would have qualified as "doctor", and they would have called me "doctor"; the same would have been true in colonial America. Hey, they call me doctor now!

I may not know all of the things that you know but I know better than to insult an educated woman who is preparing for childbirth. This was an MBA here.

Get with the program, David, you are here to support your wife. I wonder if the whole meaning of my existence was to be here for her.

The kids would say, "Us too," and I would say, well, yes, that's part of it. I did have something to do with that.

I could tell you a story about the Buxton Inn in Ohio... but that's a digression, the point is that we were dutifully and fearfully attending Lamaze training.

Counting and breathing. Practicing not lying flat. Practicing walking. We were champs at walking. And we heard suggestions about eating Chinese food and driving on bumpy country roads, but those suggestions were not delivered in Lamaze class.

Chinese food actually played another role in the birth of our second child who was also past due for her birthdate. Karen's fortune cookie said, "A delay is better than a disaster." We have had some awesome and spooky fortune cookies over the years.

We were scared and we were serious and we were determined. No one expressed confidence and assurance. No one offered intervention or support, either. I would say that there was a general sense of calm indifference, if that's even a category. I generally got remarks to the effect of "take this seriously" and "pay attention to Karen", and she encountered something along the lines of "that sounds nice". Placid indifference? Is that a category?

It began to seem a little lonely except that we were in a very active church and our doctor was Mike Marsh, a fellow church member and elder at the church where I was preaching as a part-time fill-in preacher, while I was also a full-time instructor at

Bridgewater College. God bless Brethren Church insurance from the college.

And the due date came and went with few false alarms. It looked as if we might spend Christmas waiting and watching. And waiting.

I really don't remember much about that December. We bought a live tree. I know that because the wood stove in the house generated so much dry heat that it killed the tree and dried it out and every needle was lying in a green circle around it when I came home after delivery. I don't remember singing or us watching Christmas movies or really much of anything except delivery.

The delivery room was very homey. It was decorated to be like a room in a home, not a clinical operating room or the kind of room the Emergency Room wards had. It had nice earthy warm colors and blankets and a cushioned chair.

And we arrived at it too early. Labor pains and contractions can be misleading. You think you're making progress. You think dilation is going great. Uphill, uphill, we're counting, and we're breathing – remember those cleansing breaths – and then you reach a plateau. Instead of getting to the top of the hill or blessedly over it to the other side, you are standing on an empty overlook of nothing much, wondering what happened.

Mike came by and checked frequently. The twenty second turned over to the twenty third, and then the twenty-fourth. Christmas cookies and egg nog lost appeal. Doctors and nurses who dropped by with those were cheerful and they probably wondered why I didn't reach out for them. It was because Karen had my hand. I don't know how long a hand can endure not having blood in it from being squeezed.

The problem may have been medication. The painkiller may have been too much for her exhaustion and it may have been putting her to sleep, and sleep, or the lack of it may have slowed labor. They gave her a painkiller and it was two mistakes – it stopped her from walking and it may have put her to sleep.

That went on for hours. And hours. And maybe even more hours.

Not to worry, pain came back with a vengeance, and I really wondered if Karen was going to break my hand. She needed to swear or bite or something, she needed to know something, she needed for me to stop explaining how the contractions looked on the monitor. My face was close to hers, partly because she had pulled me there. I don't think my arm was breaking yet, at that point. I could feel how tense she was and how tired and frustrated she was. Were we at twenty-six hours in that delivery room? And she said, "Tell me something else! Get my mind off this! Please!"

And that was when I asked her if she remembered Hong Kong. I couldn't see the monitor anymore. I couldn't see the curves and lines of the contractions. I couldn't tell about the peaks and valleys any more. I don't even remember the beeping. But I could sense that her body seemed suddenly different. Words like lighter and easier don't make sense. Maybe a flow of energy would make more sense. Maybe a new flow of life like a wave would describe it. She was remembering and loving Hong Kong.

And I asked her if she remembered the ride on the tram and she smiled… until she pressed her chin into her chest again and turned red and spat out a breath or a swear word… her mind was on the tram. I talked about every foot of that ride. The clear day. The people who were there. The peak of Victoria. The overlooks. The view. The rooftops and terraces. The harbor breeze. The fragrant harbor.

Her memories were so vivid and her love for it so intense that she responded to that story as labor intensified. And before five o'clock on Christmas Eve our first baby was born. You could say that Sarah Lambert was born on a virtual tram ride up Victoria Peak.

Our Baby, she was bare headed bald when she was born, maybe there was a hint of her bright red hair but a hint would be all. Her little bright eyes were already open and alert and searching the world. She was happy to be with her parents.

I had been watching shows and reading about bonding and from the first moments of holding her I felt a bond. Hers was a little life that was an extension of mine and mine was part of hers. We shared life. We shared comfort and contentment and joy. She laughed. In her first moments of living she laughed as some of her first sounds.

There, if you want to call it this, was the magic of Christmas. Peace, joy, hope, and love, a little light, a little pale candle flame on Christmas Eve.

What a birthdate.

I suppose that it's a bummer to a kid to have a Christmas Eve birthday.

We saddled her with a double name because of a family of girls with double names at our wedding. They were our friends through college and church, through our times in choir and after college, and we promised that someday we too would name all our girls with double names. It seemed so genteel and southern. We wanted to honor and preserve family names, so Karen chose her grandmother, Cordie Sarah Lambert Harris Bradley. The Lamberts and the Mims were important ancestors to Karen. So we settled on Sarah Lambert. We knew she was a girl from the first ultrasound exam.

She had to stay in the hospital an extra day or two to be treated for jaundice. She really was carrot color then, or maybe pumpkin color.

Once she was over that, and a normal hue, we could take her home. We had researched the correct car seat, learned how to strap it in. I scraped the frosty morning ice from the car and ran the heater in hopes that I could get its interior to match the temperature of the hospital. We carried her out, bundled in blankets and carefully drove our precious cargo home. We'd made a nursery upstairs with a Jenny Lind cradle and a Jenny Lind changing table. That room was mostly sunlight and wood grains.

Not everything was pink. Some things were pale blue, but it was baby blue and didn't necessarily label itself as "boy" or exclude

139

her, but most things were pink or pale yellow. One of my students from Spain, Paula Artal-Isbrand, herself an artist and art historian and archaeologist, knitted her a fine yellow sweater. Receiving blankets became special things. I kept some for years as if they were sacred objects, but they probably got called into duty as the next five came along.

Since her birthday on that Christmas Eve in 1987, she has swum in the frigid water in Iceland, snorkeling between the continents underwater along the mid-Atlantic ridge, walked the inter-community trails between towns and villages in Germany, shopped in the Christmas markets, sipped gluhwein, she's hiked the Alps, she wandered on the Isle of Skye, had colors poured over her during Holi in India, danced in a Bollywood style saree dress for Sangeet at her sister's Indian wedding in India, visited the Taj Mahal, attended college, acted in Arsenic and Old Lace, won numerous state medals in forensics, won medals in art, petted hedgehogs in Japan, driven rings around Italy, sat in a window in

Florence, crossed the wall of the Vatican, and crawled through prehistoric cairns.

She beats me all hollow as an artist and always has, especially as her own businesswoman and entrepreneur. Her Etsy shop made twice as much money when she was 22 as I earned when I was 30 teaching college. Her ideas for how to run an online art business have attracted friends to her from many corners of the U.S. and all walks of life, seeking her insights, input and advice.

The loving and giving Sarah Lambert. She came home from Kindergarten and told me verbatim the story from Shel Silverstein's The Giving Tree. That Christmas, at age five, she sang a solo of One Small Child to an audience of more than two hundred in the auditorium of the church and school in Virginia.

Credits to David Meece, born 1952, his copyright song:

"One small child in a land of a thousand,

One small dream of a savior tonight.

One small hand reaching out to the starlight,

One small savior of life."

That little brave red-haired girl sang it clearly, loudly and flawlessly on a stage in front of all those people.

What a gift a birth is, what gifts a little life brings.

One small hand reaching out to the starlight...

Chapter Nine

Mountains and Valleys

Karen loves the mountains almost as much as she loves anyone, and she keeps wanting to get back to them.

In the early morning before daylight the silhouettes of the trees show their shapes. The black verticals, their spreading limbs, they look like motifs for the unwritten day.

On a hot summer day the pine straw smells as strong as brewing coffee in a beanery.

The black soil crumbles richly in your fingers like coffee grounds.

The trail crunches beneath your feet, in the caked dry summer and in the frothy layers of winter snow.

Karen said that when she was a teenager her family rode horses up Mount LeConte in the Great Smoky Mountains, beside the columns of pines and firs and hemlocks to the grassy dome that overlooks Gatlinburg and Pigeon Forge and eastern Tennessee, and she wanted to go back there and do that horse ride to the lodge again someday.

We hiked up that trail many times but we never faced the further effort to the mountain top; we only went as far as Alum Cave Bluffs, passed little cascading waterfalls so loud you think you're hearing a party of people laugh and mingle when you're really alone. The Mountain Laurels and Rhododendrons reach out thick green leaves, clapping their hands as you parade past them up the path.

For many people, a vacation in the mountains would mean sitting in a rocking chair just gazing out at the treetops. We did that once or twice at a place called The Wonderland Hotel in the Smokies. The Wonderland, the old original one is gone now, but we used to love it and the stream near it.

But it was never enough of a vacation to us to just sit and contemplate, we had to be exploring and hiking and seeing things we hadn't seen before, or revisiting trails and streams we had seen and loved. Sunlight and shadow, walking on the dappled trails, sometimes in ribbons and rays, sometimes marveling as the sunshine lit the transparent leaves yellow-green like fine gossamer fans against the dark contrast of the forests. Water on ferns, water dripping from rocks, and water on webs like strings of bright pearls strung for the elegance and enchantment of the woodlands. Rhododendron and Mountain Laurel and Trillium and other flowers – you learn things, bit by bit as you live around mountains and explore trails. When we lived in The Shenandoah Valley we learned about Trillium, the little triangles of white, and their gentle reminder of the harmonic math of the universe just mingling there amid the green.

We lived in "The Valley" fourteen years, and sometimes we have thought of Shenandoah as the river, sometimes we thought of it as the scenery along Interstate 81, and sometimes we thought of it as the region from Roanoke south of us to Woodstock to our north. Sometimes we thought of it as the name of the wind or perhaps the song the wind sings. Most of the time we thought of the mountains when we thought about the valley, of Shenandoah National Park and its waterfalls and hiking trails, of the Blue Ridge that looks like a nappy old rug piled indifferently in a corner for the winter. Those wrinkles and crumples are forests and hollows with names like Limberlost and Lewis, White Oak Canyon and Dark Hollow. Above them rocks rise up like teeth from ancient and tired jaws. Bear Fence. Old Stony Man. To the south are Humpback Rocks and The Peaks of Otter. The great divide is Afton Mountain.

There is no such thing as an unsentimental recognition of those mountains. There is no cool unemotional strictly scientific way to talk about them. In a way, they are like a single animal organism with a complex set of personalities and multiple names. In another way, they are like a family or a clan, with separate habitats yet all related. Their Appalachian cousins are the Smokies in North Carolina and Tennessee, their roots are in Georgia, and

146

their toes nudge Alabama at places with names like Rising Fawn. West of them the Alleghenies take up a rivalry into Pennsylvania and a proud character of mountaineers and mountain fish and the palisades of trees that once cradled the forts of the western frontier. You are right in thinking that was long ago, before the nation had a name; but even after the United States had a Constitution that mountain region west of Virginia and Maryland, across western Pennsylvania and Ohio was still called "the frontier".

Even a mountain trail can be a walk through time and an examination of the past.

I used to tell Karen to imagine it all as George Washington saw it as a scout, when he tramped his way west to the territory that would become Ohio, before Daniel Boone courted Rebecca Bryan and walked to the Cumberland Gap and Kentucky, before Washington clumsily started The French-Indian War, before he carved his initials in the stone bridge, Natural Bridge south of Lexington, before there was a Rockbridge County or a Rockingham

County, before German farmers brought Amish and Mennonite names like Yoder to the highways and mills, when it was all green and virgin forests. It is still surprisingly simple to imagine that.

One other place where we were able to envision the not so distant past like that was at Pawnee Rock in Kansas. It is easy to look out from the watchtower there and imagine the herds of bison that blackened that flat cocoa brown dirt and bent the tall grass prairie, especially if you walked upon "the buffalo steps" the herds left behind. And those years and those pioneers were not as far distant from our lives as the ones who first walked across The Valley. And in neither place, not Virginia or Kansas, were the pioneers the first people to cross the land or to settle it. The Shenandoah Valley had been prepared hunting ground by Native Americans for centuries. That was why those fields were so attractive to the farmers. The same was true in Kansas. The names the farmers brought to the Arkansas River Valley in Kansas were the same as in Shenandoah too, like Yoder.

Karen would enjoy the words and names in those places as heartily as she would inhale the fresh wind. Perhaps Shenandoah is a great spirit. Or a fragrance. The aroma of life, fertility, the beckoning love of open arms and fresh springs. The Mississippi River is "the father of waters", then perhaps Shenandoah is a mother. Like a mother you want to go back to her. Her foods are the tastiest, her songs the sweetest. You have things you want to tell her and show her. You don't want her to change. You would like to find the same mother waiting for you every time you came home.

The soil in the Shenandoah Valley is rich and black; pick it up and it explodes with life. The wind gathered it and brought it there and spread it like a gift. Floods deposited it. Winds spread it.

It may seem like all that we did with that fertile dirt of the valley was walk on it, but we did plant a garden, too, a nice garden of which we were very proud, behind our rented house in Bridgewater. We had a grape arbor, started by some previous resident in the succession of people that lived there on one of the oldest farm plots next to the Brethren church at the corner of Bridgewater College. There were brick pillars of the old college gates in Bridgewater right next to the house, columns that our two girls climbed up and down because they were situated so close to us that they were too tempting and seemed like part of our property. That was the lawn with the stone boat; but it was never our property, we just rented it for a while.

When we moved to Virginia, the mountains were our first challenges. Could we do it? Could we walk from the parkway all the way down White Oak Canyon and back again? It was a scary consideration. Do we need backpacks? Do we need the correct shoes? Would we dehydrate?

Up there on those trails we learned about blazes. They come in many colors. They come in many colors because many trails cross and parallel and diverge up there. We learned to read there, in our twenties, the alphabets and grammar of the woodlands. We learned to read the blazes so that we wouldn't be lost, and we would know which trail we were on, where it came from and where it was going.

The Appalachian Trail is sort of an artery and sort of a spine because the mountains themselves are sort of a backbone, and sometimes best described like fingers; they wend their way in bewildering patterns that defy the cardinal points of the compass. Northeast and southwest are as important to find as true north and the stars.

This chapter, all of these words would all be fine with Karen, all this waxing eloquent about the mountains, because she loves those mountains. There are not many ways to make her eyes glisten or see her get dreamily lost in reveries, yet those places can do it. There is always a tug to "Get back there".

There's a bit of a contradiction in how we started, veering toward the mountains or migrating someplace else. It was water versus woodlands, sort of. I am a water person. I am as attracted to water as iron is to a magnet. I could probably rent myself out as divining rod, a dowsing stick. It didn't surprise me at all to find out that Thor and Thorasson are my ancestors, it rains wherever I go.

I've kidded all the children for years that we should just advertise

ourselves as rainmakers. When we moved to Georgia we broke a

ten-year drought with a record flood. Before I met Karen I was a

constant swimmer. I was never any good at it, but I could spend all

day and all night in the water. I figured out as a teenager that I am

healthiest if I periodically stand in the rain or walk in the rain. I took

"Sailing" as my P.E. in college. So, naturally, I wanted to go to the

beach.

I was so known for swimming at night that when a local boy

drowned one summer midnight I found out the next day that the

college I attended had spent the following morning closing out my

records because when they heard of a drowning on the radio they

just assumed it was me.

The lakes, the beach, the water... boats, the tide, the

waves...

Karen would have none of it.

She wouldn't go to the beach, she doesn't like hot weather, she doesn't want to bask in the sun, don't suggest a Caribbean honeymoon, her favorite James Bond movie is not Thunderball, she won't go fishing (yet)... it was not until after the birth of our second child that I talked her into going to The Outer Banks of North Carolina and that was a trip in search of history, which she loves, and the Cape Hatteras lighthouse, and Blackbeard.

She loves the mountains.

Even when our pockets were empty I could easily talk her into a drive to the mountains and a hike. We have gone to Gatlinburg flat broke more times than we've ever gone and bought tickets at the attractions.

Even a beggar can walk in the woods. A mountain meadow is The Court of Miracles.

There are places along Skyline Drive, the highway through the Shenandoah National Park, that I called "The Cathedrals of Trees". The branches of the trees along that road stretch across it to meet as pointed arches shading tunnels of green and making stripes of sunlight like great green vaulted ribs, a construction Abbot Suger, architect of a cathedral in Paris would envy.

I can't remember which trail in the Shenandoah National Park was our first trail, Dark Hollow Falls or South River Falls. Dark Hollow was always attractive because it was easy and in remembering the trail it always seemed short. It's not so short. Each of those trails takes no less than an hour, and realistically a hiker should devote half a day, three to four hours, to get to a waterfall and back and be able to leisurely enjoy the forest and the trail. South River, on the other hand, never seemed short but it seemed cool and dark and shady with a variety of wonders. There is a place along the path of South River Falls where you can hear the water running and gurgling under your feet, beneath the rocks that are like flagstones. You can hear it, but you can't see it, and you know that you will meet it further on, like a game of lost and found and hide and seek between you and the mountain. White Oak Canyon trail became our favorite, with its long walk through the hemlocks of The Limberlost and the trek along the rocks to cliffs and streams, through much variety and wonder. If you hike White Oak Canyon from the parkway all the way down to the eastern base of the mountains and then back up again that is quite a summer day's stretch.

Get back there.

This is like "A Tale of Two Parks", the Shenandoah National Park and the Great Smoky Mountains National Park. I keep wanting to write about place names and campgrounds and tell stories, and thrill over seeing elk return to Oconaluftee. That was sheer joy to see the return of the elk, like hugging and embracing someone. It's always a joy to us when we drive through Cherokee, North Carolina, to the Oconaluftee entrance to The Great Smokies, like a kind of homecoming, like we ought to shout, "We're back!"

Go back there.

Yes, like a magnet to iron, we're drawn back. When can we go back? Can we plan a camping trip? It seems like Karen is always planning a camping trip or thinking of one, investigating another campground, checking rates.

To get ready for our first camping trips together we searched ads in the local papers and found a couple in Waynesboro that were selling their tents and cots. We hung around the campsites of friends to pick up tips. In our mid-twenties we were beginners. Novice campers. Tenderfoots. "That's tender feet."

Get back there.

So many places. So many memories. Hot Springs, Virginia. Douthat State Park near Hot Springs. Some of those places are state parks, not in either of the national parks. Some are places that border the national forests; places like McKinley, Virginia, south of Staunton, where Dr. Scott Smith's farm, Leeward Acres, backed up to the edge of tall trees that skirted the national forest.

He was our friend, Dr. Smith, he and his wife, Tess. They invited us to visit them and stay at their place as some of the first people to welcome us to Virginia. We arrived in Virginia in a blizzard in early February 1983. This is not an exaggeration, it was a record one day snowfall, and I had rarely ever even seen snow, and never more than two inches; that snowfall was two feet. And we moved from Mississippi to Virginia to get there just in time for that.

Scott Smith retired from the U.S. Navy out of Norfolk. He served in World War II in Leyte Gulf and told me stories – some of them about ghastly wounds that led him to become an oral surgeon. He was a tall and sort of gangly fellow from Pennsylvania, and he wanted to breed horses as a hobby.

We had a connection to Norfolk in Becky Sporhase who took my place as art teacher in the missionary school in Papua New Guinea. Her parents, also retired Navy, showed us around Norfolk and went with us to the Chrysler Museum of Art. The Sporhases and Smiths attended Tabernacle Church in Norfolk ("Tab" they called it) and they had already discussed the Cooks, these young missionaries, who were moving to Virginia.

There have never ever been two warmer and more welcoming people that meant so much to two crazy young strangers.

Get back there.

There was a fresh water spring in Leeward Acres, Dr. Smith's farm, and it fed a trickling brook that wended its way past the house to the road. I used to drink up that spring from a ladle. Now, sitting here, I don't know why I didn't fill gallons with that water to take home to our apartment back then. Stupid me. Well, we didn't drink bottled water in those days; we didn't bottle water very often, either. Maybe we filled a thermos or a canteen, once in a while, because dehydration was always a concern. I had a plastic folding camping cup that I used to fill with water trickling over rocks along Dark Hollow and White Oak Canyon. If the streams cascaded and aerated enough through brushy clumps of grasses I would reach into the creeks and fill my cup. That was a risk. Signs everywhere warned of e.coli, abundant e.coli, and the dangers of bacteria. I was casual about it because I had been treated so much for dysentery in Papua New Guinea that I was recklessly unafraid.

That's why anglers used to carry whiskey, as a disinfectant of course, and where the saying, "bourbon and branch water" came from. I had the branch water, but darn it I never had the bourbon.

Karen would get glowing red, hiking those trails. For years we were as thin as twigs, until we started competing for food against babies. After that you learn to wolf down your food with one hand out ready for danger and a cautious eye on lookout. Eating what the kids eat makes you fat.

Eating the diet of the dollar store and food bank isn't so good, either.

We inadvertently terrified Nathan when he was a toddler. We would say that we were going to the mountains "for a long explore" and we acted so excited and happy about it and made a special point of it that we were taking him along and we were taking him "for a long explore". That's right, we were cheerfully and sweetly quoting A.A. Milne and that Tigger book, and he was dreadfully associating it, which we were not doing. We were quoting Milne without thinking about quoting Milne, thinking we were taking him for a joyous ride and a jaunty tour of the mountains and woods we all loved so much, and he was thinking that we were taking him to leave him, and lose him and teach him a lesson, whereby he would become "a sad Tigger, a sorry Tigger, a Rabbit I'm so glad to see you Tigger."

We wondered why he seemed so nervous and excitable in the car, why he was so restless and stir crazy on a drive that we had to fuss, why he was tugging and clinging, why his eyes were wide and darting and he seemed afraid on the daylight trail. I can't remember whether he told us right then and there, or whether he told us oh so much too much later, but there can be a lot of guilt and forehead slapping as a parent.

There were several times when friends thought we were risking killing them, like the time we found ourselves atop Little

Stony Man during a solar eclipse we didn't know was coming and we wondered how quickly hypothermia could set in wearing shorts and t-shirts as the temperature plunged in the dark. There was the time we led two carloads of friends down White Oak Canyon without realizing it would be dark, completely dark, pitch dark, long before we got back to the cars. We were rescued by seeing headlights from the parking lot just as we were running desperately up while we could still tell there was a trail. There were steep cliffs we forgot about. And there were rattlesnakes. Once Sarah Lambert and I encountered a black bear while she was in a carrier on my back and I was explaining to her how you could tell what animals had been on the trail, and how long before, by reading their droppings. Oh, look, Sarah Lambert, this must have been a bear. Then I heard its warning growl. It wasn't actually on the trail, it was farther down the slope to our left, but we could see the shine on its fur just beyond the thicket. Obviously we made it out unharmed.

I used to tease Katy Lynn on walks, "Don't step on my shadow!", and she would and I would yell "ouch!" and she would giggle and laugh and I would say, "You are my shadow." I know we borrowed the nickname, and she did too, to call her Scout.

Karen and I finally hiked up Mount LeConte together, all the way to the peak, to stay overnight in a cabin. They don't do the same trail ride that Karen took with her parents, not anymore, but we could still spend a night in a cabin, and we could still eat with everyone in the large dining hall; much of it had remained the same, including warnings to be wary and watchful for black bears.

The trail to Mont LeConte is an easy walk at first toward Alum Cave Bluffs. We've taken babies and children up that path. There's not much danger to the stream. It gets a bit trickier and a little scarier after you cross at a hole through a rock up stone steps, especially in icy months of winter. Icicles sometimes fall in sheets and spears from the bluffs. The dirt and gravel of the path make slippery and unsure footing even in the driest times, and the loose dirt at the bluffs is really difficult to walk on. Beyond the bluffs the real walk up the mountain begins through shadows, mists and fog, on the lookout for bears, wondering if you have brought the wrong snacks, the kinds that bears can smell, the kinds that bears really like. Roots in the path and along it can trip you up if you don't watch your feet, but who can keep their eyes on their feet when the trees and mountainsides are so breathtaking to look at?

Just measuring by "favorite pictures" as a gauge, as in numbers of pictures and how many have become computer wallpapers and smartphone screens, Karen's favorite places are The Chimney Tops and Alum Cave Bluffs – not the "chimney" rocks themselves, they petrify us and threaten us with vertigo – Karen loves the clear water stream and big boulders in the stream at Chimney Tops and she loves the rock tunnel up the stone steps at Alum Cave Bluffs.

Over the years you come to appreciate the Civilian Conservation Corps and all that they did and you wish they would reassemble and do it some more. For people who love history, the CCC and all that they accomplished and what they left us becomes a cherished study. State parks like Vogel in Georgia, on the other side of Blood Mountain, just the other side of the Appalachian Trail below Neels Gap, as well as national parks like The Great Smokies are their museums and their memorials and we all owe them and Franklin Delano Roosevelt a great debt. Herbert Hoover doesn't come off so badly, either, when you explore the Shenandoah parks and Camp Hoover.

Many times that I've been fly fishing I've thought about Hoover. Before him, Teddy Roosevelt and John Muir and the photographer William Henry Jackson and the painter Thomas Moran and you realize that we do indeed travel on the backs of others, perhaps we should say "on the shoulders of giants", at least in their shadows and on their footprints.

Chapter Ten

Process

Circling and circling, what's your process?

A few drops of water on the suzuri, the grinding stone for

sumi ink, and then you press the ink stick to the stone and water,

circling and circling, round and round until the water has become

thick black ink. Then you draw with the brush, the fine tip making

the tiny start of the line, and turn the bristles to make the wide fat

of the line. In your picture, can you count the five tones?

What is your process?

How do you put a jigsaw puzzle together? Do you start

with the edge pieces that have one straight side? Or start with a

color and gather all the pieces of that color? Or do you search for

patterns or details and piece them together?

How do you play the game? Do you read the instructions first? Or do you plunge in and let the other players explain it as you go? Do you amass your pieces? Do you build an army? Buy a country? Do you try to own part of the board? And when you play chess, are you trying to win the center? Get your pieces out of the back, in front of the pawns to maximize them? Do you spend your concentration trying to protect your queen? Are you trying to defend your king or capture the other?

Could you spend an hour finding out how a roof is thatched? Would you give that a day, even if you don't own one, just out of curiosity to know how it's done?

When you pick up the knitted sweater in the department store, do you already know how it was made?

How to do the thing can be as exciting as the thing itself. Surely it's part of it.

A pocket watch isn't just a pocket watch, it had to be made.

This family is not a team; eight people think they are captain and there seem to be three or four commissioners in the wings.

I asked Nathan what it is like to work with his mother on editing what he writes.

"She likes to talk about process. She wants to know about intention and get an idea of what you plan and where you are going. She wants each thing to be productive.

"Mom really thinks through a problem. She goes right to the best questions first. She has the questions that are really going to get things done.

"The way she comments is really good because she sees the flaws, they bother her. She gets mad where the logic falls apart. She gets mad at logical absurdities. She would make a great comedian because she sees where it falls apart, she sees the breaks and leaps in logic."

Karen will say, "That doesn't make sense," and she gets frustrated when a character or a plot go off in some direction that seems out of step with where they were going. She can be that way in everyday life as much as react that way to fiction.

"Why did they think that? Why did they do that? Why did they say that?"

"Why?," is a valid question to ask. Why is important to understand.

Research, research, research, let's have this well planned and studied. Let's read.

Someone told me once, kind of exasperatedly, "You can't learn to ride a horse reading a book."

Uh, plenty of people have learned to do things watching YouTube, why not from reading a book?

Her uncle George Hoak in Atlanta had a store in Stone Mountain called Memorable Books and he filled the basement of his house with books just as he filled shelves and shelves along every available wall and space.

"Read any good books lately?" George would ask in his New York accent.

Karen loves books. When we lived in Virginia we would go to the Green Valley Book Fair. That's where we found The Timetables of History. Our world has been filled with memorable names of bookstores: Lemuria books in Jackson, Mississippi, The Book Rack, Memorable Books in Stone Mountain, The Royal Oak Bookshop in Front Royal, Virginia. Places with new books and used books, books to order and books that were secondhand. We have spent a lot of time searching for books, searching through books, and reading. And you can't just read it, you have to discuss it.

She persuaded me to read Arms and the Man, and she told me all about The Lady is Not for Burning, the Christopher Fry play, calling it "The Witch is Not for Burning", so it took me a while to find it.

I can't remember the first time that Karen mentioned The Tinderbox and the hound whose eyes were as big as saucers. She heard Anderson's fairy tales and Grimm's fairy tales from her Grandma and Grandpa Blake. I couldn't tell how many times Karen has told "The Tinderbox" and "The Twelve Dancing Princesses".

I remember her searching for some of Dorothy Dunnet's books, *The Lymond Chronicles*. She was enthralled by that series. I don't know how many paperback copies we have of those.

"What do you like in those books?" I asked.

"The male protagonist is usually a flawed character, not well understood by the people around him. His motives might be called into question.

"Hornblower is not understood. He isn't knowable. He isn't understood by the people around him. Maybe it's because he keeps things to himself.

"The woman – I wouldn't be looking for that, not the same thing. I'm usually looking for a woman with a lot of initiative, someone who has to step out and figure something out, has to figure out how to get it done, how to accomplish what's needed."

She read a lot of Mary Stewart books. "Tons of them. A whole bunch."

She is often intrigued by time travel. The movie, Somewhere in Time, has a pocket watch that one character hands to the other with the words, "Come back to me." The man goes back in time a few decades and gives that woman the watch. It's a loop then, you see, of each one giving the other one that watch. It drove Karen crazy. Where did the watch come from, then? Where did it start? How was it ever made?

Oh, and of course, a watch is a time piece. "A time piece," get it?

A watch is a thing that has to be made. Someone made it. There was a process.

She is more interested in a single protagonist than in a couple or a group.

"What about Nick and Nora Charles?"

"Yeah, what about 'em? Oh, they're clever. I like the witty banter. It's not a very involved mystery, though, is it?"

Eudora Welty lived around the corner from me in Belhaven. She waved from her upstairs window, once or twice, and always smiled. I spoke to her often at the Jitney Jungle grocery store and Parkin's Pharmacy. I carried her groceries a couple of times.

Do you remember Miss Welty's story "Why I Live at the P.O."?

I regularly tell the girls that I am going to run away to the YMCA. "Why I Live at The Y", will one day be my future story. Eh, I don't have to run away to the Y, I could just sail off on a boat.

Does everyone have to talk at once? Do we have to have three conversations crossing over each other and across the table and across the room, all at once?

One starts talking, then another starts talking, then the first one objects to being interrupted while the second one is still talking, and the third one wants a word in edgewise, and the fourth one gets incensed and wants to defend the first one while trying to follow the second one's point, and I will probably be criticized for not listening or caring or refereeing. I was pretty sure that someone in there asked a question, and I thought I had a couple of opinions that I wanted to offer.

They sure can argue! I quote from The Princess Bride: "You hear that, princess? Those are the shrieking eels?" And I mean them.

I sound like Mr. Darling in *Peter Pan*, "A little less noise, please, a little less noise."

And Dr. Seuss's Grinch, "Oh, the noise, Noise, NOISE!"

And I turn to process and meditation.

You know, the samurai invented haiku poetry as a means to calm down.

By the way, do you pronounce caramel as "car-mul" or "care-mell"?

"I hate you, Daddy! You're such a meanie!"

How can I concentrate on writing? Worse yet, how can I focus on editing?

My method of writing is sort of like a journalist's. I write something so that I get out what is in my head, whatever constitutes my understanding of a thing, and have something sprawled out there on the page. Maybe there are ribs, maybe there is a backbone, and perhaps I've got the heart or the skin of it. I may have it turned around. I often think of Ezra Pound's "I Gather the Limbs of Osiris." Putting it together, bit by bit. Whatever it is it's never enough, it isn't in the right place, and I can't be sure that it is whole and correct. So then I go and interview and ask questions and get some dialogue. Then I go back and write some more, maybe even write the rest. Chances are I have more editing and fleshing out and interviewing to do. Back and forth, I go, until it's done or it is passed along.

So, I say to Karen, I need to ask you some more questions.

She says, "I will sit down side by side with you. You can have your copy open and I'll have one and I'll show you my edits and ideas. I'll show them to you. I've done this with Nathan. It's easy."

I say that that is not my method. I say that my method is to ask questions, like an interview, and get some more answers and material and go back and write some more, and then maybe come back for more. And so on...

"We'll do it my way," she says. "This is good. It will be fun."

I go upstairs and have some aspirin... and some ibuprofen.

Nathan realized that he was a writer in elementary school. He loves words and phrases. You can treat him with an interesting word, like rewarding someone with candy, and he savors it. He started an ambitious epic back then which I will not divulge, and he started it way back before middle school was done.

Nathan loved Robert Louis Stevenson early. He enlightened me as to the real nature and hypocrisy of Dr. Jekyll, told me Stevenson's life story in better depth than I had cursorily grasped, and loved that little epitaph poem of Stevenson's about, "Home is the sailor, home from the sea, and the hunter home from the hill." He got to work in the restaurant that is in the haunted Pirates House in Savannah, Georgia, the very place that inspired Stevenson's Treasure Island. He thinks something grabbed his foot once, in the lower depths of the house, in the dark passageway. Better not go down there again, it's dark.

They read, they talk, they edit.

Listen, Karen cheats at reading books; she reads the last chapter first, to make her mind up about the book. Or so she says. She wants to know where it's going, whether reading will be worth it. Perhaps she just can't stand the suspense. The last chapter first, but never the first chapter last?

She denies this!

"Don't be ridiculous. I always look at the first chapter first!"

Don't make her angry.

"I always read the beginning first!" she shouts, and she looks very upset.

"It's only certain books where I look at the end. Romance books, I do that with romance books."

She adamantly denies this.

I have treated her scandalously, I can tell.

She can dwell on details and she doesn't want them left out and she demands that they be accurate.

If you want to talk about phenomenology then you'd better go to a different café because dwelling on every sip and savor isn't going to get us anywhere.

A life that's fully lived is making progress. See where you are and know where you're going. Purpose. Plan. Intention.

I don't know why anyone would ever think that we are undisciplined. Maybe we seem too confident, relaxed and casual.

Are you at work, Karen?

"Of course I am. Don't be ridiculous."

Grandpa Blake would joke about his wife, saying, "There she is, Lucille Blake, the girl of wonders; she often wonders."

The wondering family. I wonder about this and I wonder about that. And isn't that a wonder?

Janet is Karen's younger sister. They wonder together.

For as long as I've known them they have been a talkative pair. When they are together I may as well depart, go fishing or get something done, because they won't even notice my absence while they talk and talk.

The kids and I have said it many times as we see Karen and Janet together. "Well, they're gone, that's that. We'll make contact again in a couple of days."

Janet's husband, Rich and I, stood at the base of part of the Alum Caves Bluff Trail on a frosty February day for what must have been an hour because unbeknownst to us Karen and Janet, talking, had wandered on up the trail and kept going to the icy bluffs. Several kids (young adults, really) were sitting in their car waiting, too.

When they are talking to each other there is no one else in their world, perhaps they aren't even in the same world as the rest of us while they talk.

They have long discussions while driving about what it means to sense something in advance of it happening. That's the literal definition of "premonition". Sensing what someone is going to say before they say it, knowing exactly what is about to come out of their mouth, and never wrong about it. Sensing in the night that someone is in trouble and she should pray for them. Wondering what that means; that what is going to happen is going to happen. What does that mean about what God is doing?

179

"If I can know the next words that are going to come out of your mouth," says Karen, "what does that mean about what is happening?"

Janet is outside of the bank worrying, conflicted about what to do next. It's a long and complicated story. A lady in a pink hat, a complete stranger wants to pray for her, the timing is incredible; they pray together. She thinks, "That nice lady was a complete stranger, I never saw her before and I'll never see her again", but only a few days later Janet runs into that same lady at a restaurant and they talk again.

Janet will wake up from a dream and think, "I need to be praying for this person," and not know why she feels that way. The next day she finds out that the person she prayed for in the night has been going through some kind of crisis – a health issue or financial distress, something – and needed prayers.

Is it inevitable? Are we part of "destiny"?

Janet doesn't dwell on it, but Karen does.

Janet puzzles over it; they both puzzle over it. They talk.

Is premonition like some kind of prophecy? Is it weird coincidence?

Karen would know, as the phone rang, who was calling before she picked up the receiver and answered it.

"If that can happen at all, what does it mean about the future?"

"It means that there is no chance at all that you will change your mind. It means that what is going to happen will happen."

We often say, "I am where I am supposed to be. I am doing what I am meant to be doing."

Chapter Eleven

Papua New Guinea

If you are going to another country across the Pacific Ocean, nine thousand miles away from home and parents, it would probably be best not to walk all day on a Hawaiian beach without sunscreen or covering and so not poison your body with sunburn to the point of being deathly sick. I am not talking about me, I could probably spend a day naked in Death Valley and not be noticeably pink. I'm talking about Karen, who my memory of her lying on a bed in Port Moresby in our first minutes in Papua New Guinea is about the same as the way a hot dog looks in a microwave oven after a minute too long. I remember desperately wondering, standing there in the missionary guest house in that far off island, Papua New Guinea, what would I do if the woman I loved and wanted to spend eternity with died in another country? How would I explain that she died from sunburn because we stopped off in Hawaii?

Some people really fret and plan their entrance. Karen doesn't often do that, but she would rather not have had that be her beginning of two years in another country. Thus was her entrance to Papua New Guinea.

The missionaries who ran the guest house in Port Moresby sat me down at the table in the kitchen while Karen languished in a guest bed. It's customary in many places and down through history to welcome strangers with food and show a little hospitality. Those people weren't letting that tradition disturb them. They decided that I probably needed to eat, but the hour was late, I obviously arrived at the wrong time and unprepared, and I was clearly suspect and negligent judging by the condition of my wife. There is no clearer way to let an American know he's not welcome than to offer him his first taste of Vegemite on hard biscuits. It was also my introduction to "biscuit" being a cookie or a cracker. I wouldn't see something like a soft fluffy biscuit again for three years.

And I wasn't welcome. Those people did not belong to the same missionary organization or "umbrella" that I was under and they thought my organization was daft and told me so, and I was certainly adding to that impression, sitting at a table in Port Moresby in a Harris Tweed jacket while my pink and purple wife was groaning in pain lying on a cot under a ceiling fan after I had unconscionably led her around the rocks of Hanauma Bay for hours in the sun before departing on an airplane for hours to a country that I knew nothing about. They wondered aloud how we had managed to get on a plane in Oahu and make it those long hours of flight to Papua New Guinea.

You know, I don't remember much else except the institutional plainness of the gray paint in the guest house and the metal blades of the ceiling fan overhead, and the ward-like rooms of "the guest house" and the first time I had ever spoken with Australians. It all had a colonial feeling like scenes of countless movies set in places that were once colonies of England or Germany, and of course Papua New Guinea had been a colony of both those countries and recently to that time had been under the dominion of Australia.

We weren't just a pair of crazy stupid kids in that instance, we were "ugly Americans", arrogant and ill prepared. The main thing I knew was that my wife was sick and miserable and I didn't know how to handle it and if there was blame I shared a hefty half of it.

Welcome to Papua New Guinea, the land with a cross of stars and a Bird of Paradise on its flag.

They had expected us but they hadn't expected us. They knew someone would pick us up and we'd fly to Ukarumpa in the highlands but they didn't know when. There would be two years of that kind of sense of time and planning. Everything was defined by the Southern Hemisphere, even the constellations in the sky, nine degrees south latitude, so we were operating on an Australian calendar, where Christmas is a summer holiday at the beach and winter comes with June. No need to worry about that southern U.S. way of suspiciously accusing as you ask, "You're not from around here, are you?" You aren't from around here and if you expect to stay you'd better keep your head up and your eyes open;

one false move, one misstep could start a war, or at the very least get you killed. No missteps allowed.

We had seen some steps. We spent four intense months living in South Central Los Angeles, the only two white people attending an African American church – and singing in the choir, as training for internationalization and cross-cultural immersion. Didn't anyone realize that we were from Mississippi? We fit right in. No worries, mate. I will never forget my awe at the women in Sunday uniforms marching into McCoy Memorial Baptist Church in South Central Los Angeles with military precision. How do you make progress when you keep touching one foot backward at the heel of the other? It defies a rational description of forward motion. But it's an awesome looking step.

Remarkably, after 38 years we will occasionally say what they prayed in their "grace" at meals, "If there is any poison in it, please don't let it hurt us."

To live in Papua New Guinea you should learn the market language, Tok Pisin, Neomelanesian Pidgin. You needed to know the consequences of accidents and neglect. You needed to know what things were taboo. A woman had to watch her step or she could cause trouble.

In Papua New Guinea women have to watch where they step because they aren't allowed to step over anything. Women were taboo, tambu, because of menstruation. The markets were arranged in rows of vegetables and fruits set upon the ground and you didn't dare step over the zucchinis to reach for the perfect squash or you would set off a reaction of horror and anger and the whole array of food would have to be thrown out. Don't step into the leaves at the cookout. Don't step across the bean rows in the garden. Don't step over someone's legs stretched out in the path.

Women followed twenty feet behind men. Men ate first. Children followed last, and toddlers were often seen dragging machetes.

Long skirts that nearly touched the ground were mandatory.

A spectacular and fierce country, Papua New Guinea. Port Moresby was known for "the death march" of soldiers who died mostly from dysentery in World War II.

I'm making it seem harsh and as if we were treated sternly, but it wasn't like that, it was all very pleasant. They were two of the most enjoyable years of our lives.

As someone said after I drove the car off a cliff, it can be a very unforgiving country.

The car off the cliff? Driving back from Goroka in the mountains on the gravelly ridge of the Goroka Highway the brakes on a borrowed car made the wheels lock and we moved like a slow motion hockey puck sideways off a bend of the road.

From the back, Karen shouted, "David, what are you doing?"

What would Karen tell, if she was writing this?

She might tell that she was treated at first as an add-on, like a tagalong. They knew what job they had for me, it was the whole reason we had traveled across the world, because they needed an art teacher in the missionary school, but they did not have a job for her at first, they figured that out after we got there. Along the way it was like, "Oh, I'm sure they'll think of something you can do once you get there." And they did. They realized that she could teach piano and music and she could be helpful in the middle school and high school.

Her favorite story to tell is how she made The Camel Run and beat all the other racers to Madang. It was a car race, not the sport of racing dromedaries, and she wasn't really a part of the official race, we passed them in the mud, actually, on the old dirt trail that crossed the Ramu River and the Markham River and the Markham River Valley, in wilderness beyond The Highland Highway. We were at least a day ahead of them into Madang.

We saw them from a mile away, brightly colored cars, branded by Camel cigarettes, covered in mud, many of them mired along the sides of the road. The drivers were in striped racing suits, some in helmets, some of the drivers with their helmets off in the heat, standing around their cars as we passed by in Land Cruisers and Range Rovers.

Years later, Range Rover had a great television commercial where two men were sitting in a tropical cantina for what appeared to be a sinister meeting. One describes the terrible conditions of the roads and the country. The other man says that he isn't afraid, he will bring his Range Rover.

"Oh, okay," says the first man, "then I'll bring the kids."

Yeah, well, we were with teenagers. Our vehicles handled it well but even they had limitations. Even in a dry season the rivers were full, if not high.

Crossing the rivers meant we had to cover the engines – especially the distributors – and be towed across by heavy machines, usually construction machines, as water lapped at the windows above the handles of the doors, our wheels underwater, aware of the risks of amoebae in the waters and angry locals who would have, if they had seen us, demanded tolls to pass through their land.

The seniors at the high school had asked for that trip, one unforgettable trek before the highways would be paved and the danger lost forever. They were right.

Once we arrived we could relax in crystal waters with stonefish, sea snakes and crocodiles and talk about exactly where it was that Michael Rockefeller disappeared and when was the last time the volcano erupted. Don't worry about the sea snakes, they have to latch on and chew, not so much strike and bite, and you don't need to worry about stonefish unless you step on one or grab one by accident. The deadliest seashell in the world, the Geography Cone, is really rare and it's the gastropod inside that's poisonous, not the shell, and they never just wash up on the beach. You probably wouldn't ever see the sharks that wander uninhibited from the Coral Sea, without a barrier reef to stop them.

There was that trip, yes, -- and then there was the time we accompanied two women translators to the beach to negotiate with the village Head Man, and those are probably our most often told tales.

There was a photograph of Karen in her ankle length skirt crossing a fallen tree that would rival any click bait about "World's Wildest Bridges".

And there were the kittens.

We had three kittens that followed us like puppies. They would meet us every afternoon at the bend of the road, watching excitedly for us to come home, and they would hop and prance behind us everywhere we stepped. Leaving them was one of the hardest things we ever had to do, and the reasons we cried and cried when we left.

I can just imagine people seeing us, landing in Honolulu, on our way back "home" to Mississippi, at the end of our adventures, standing in the island known for fun and leisure, crying like we'd been punished.

"Why are those two young people crying so hard on a trip to Hawaii? What happened to them? Should we ask and see?" We cried and cried so much because we left our kittens.

Three things hit us all at once on our way back to The United States, as we landed again in Hawaii: exhaustion, vertigo, and leaving the cats.

There are so many photographs of Karen in the Highlands of Papua New Guinea! Pictures of her at the Sing-Sing, photos on the Madang road, pictures of her with backdrops of the kunai grass and poinsettias and jungle trails, pictures at music recitals, at markets, with villagers, with her language translation partners, at the coffee plantation, and with those cats.

What would I say distinguished Karen in that far flung island nation? She was calm and happy and rational and sensible and sane.

Some of the members of our Bible study group decided that Christians should not communicate with unbelievers. Uh, didn't that violate the very reasons we were there?

Karen studied and communicated the facts from doctrines as well as scriptures as to why that should not be our position toward our neighbors.

A man and wife in our second study group decided that their dreams revealed their true purposes and that they should pursue the forbidden romances they experienced in dreams, essentially advocating for open marriage in the compound of a few hundred people.

Karen listened and tried her best to be an understanding friend but had many good reasons why that was not a good idea in that place at that time as missionaries.

The Cargo Cult had risen with a Head Man in a neighboring village where one of our friends was a translator. We learned all about The Cargo Cult, which could teach us all a few things in other settings, too. She was supportive of him and we prayed that the villagers would not assassinate him and his family, and for the decision that they might have to make to leave for their own safety.

Papua New Guinea has the Wontok system which is like a familial obligation. I'm not sure that anyone in western culture can really grasp it or explain it, we certainly don't seem to live it here. Karen lives it. We've had some friends, especially as a young couple in Virginia, who treated us like Wontoks. Karen is an embodiment of it: mother, sister, church member, community member, loyal coworker, wife, friend, wontok.

The only way to bathe was from a bucket shower, like two years of camping. Water gathered in a tank on the roof in rainy season and supplied us for the year, as long as there was a sufficient rainy season. We came to practice water conservation and appreciate the treasure of potable water.

Bacteria could be anywhere, in water, in the wind kicking up the dust of the dirt roads, on vegetables from market, on fruit from the trees. Karen scratched an itchy bite and her leg swelled up twice its regular diameter. That was the second time that I worried that she might die.

We made homemade ginger beer in the cola bottles left over from the grocery. Add a raisin, everyone said, and the caps popped off like little toy cannons.

They had a cookbook made by the missionaries with recipes and instructions for nearly everything and substitutes for ingredients you couldn't obtain in remote locations, such as the deep jungle. The Jungle Camp Cookbook became The Cooking Bible for Life in our house. What could we substitute if there were no eggs? What can you use if you can't get vanilla? It seems like the only irreplaceable things were chocolate chips and if the grocery didn't get them in its shipment then there was nothing... nothing... Life isn't worth living without chocolate.

There are 900 language groups in Papua New Guinea, and while Karen was there they had nine hundred and one.

There was a library in Ukarumpa, on a hill, and at that time we all had access. It wasn't a lending library, per se, it was part of the translation headquarters and the stock of books was an international range and eclectic. We read a lot of mysteries: Marjorie Allingham, Dorothy L. Sayers, and Agatha Christie. I read the Thurber books I had never seen before, quoting The Wonderful O to amuse everyone.

"I don't like it, I don't like it," skwawked the parrot, so Black scrucked his thrug until all he could whupple was "geep". "Geep", whuppled the parrot.

There was no television. There were occasionally radio stations. There was a highland newspaper with Isuzu Lou cartoons. We played board games. We played Uno and Skip Bo. Sometimes we spent days playing Avalon Hill strategy games like "Kingmaker".

On some Saturdays and Sundays there were softball games and tennis matches on clay courts.

Young men played cricket on the soccer field at the school.

We listened to a lot of music. The Corries, the Robert Shaw Chorale, Sons of the Pioneers. Bob and Sue Mahaffey shared their collections of tapes with us. Graduates of the same college, alumni together, and consequently alumni of Wycliffe. They gave their sons milk biscuits, which I am telling you is the way to turn a person away from milk forever.

The only way to have milk in Papua New Guinea was powdered milk. Some things should never be made with powdered milk because you have to add sugar to make it palatable. Mac and cheese are no good with powdered milk. Yuck. Hamburger Helper is really stinky and terrible on powdered milk.

Mac McClendon in the house next to us grew pineapples and took us motorbike riding.

Graham and Margaret James from New Zealand visited us with their children several times in the states. Margaret, ever the "take charge this needs to be done and these poor people shouldn't be left to suffer for a minute" type, found us a place to live in Ukarumpa, with banana trees and a vegetable garden and a bucket shower. They shared the architecture and culture of New Zealand with us.

We watched the storms come over the grassy mountains from our back steps, sometimes foolishly. A lightning strike behind our house one evening stunned us so badly we could barely think and move, but we were still breathing.

Karen delighted in seeing and being near "the flying foxes", the giant bats. We got fish and chips, once, in Lae, and went to a park on the coast where you could watch the bats return to the fruit trees at sunset. She was thrilled, not afraid.

Is Karen brave? She certainly is daring. She dared the dangers of South Central Los Angeles and Watts, she dared the unknown of Papua New Guinea, she climbed the mountain to see what was on the other side, and she tasted foods she wasn't weaned on.

She rescued me from a dog attack – a huge vicious American Staffy, estimated at 80 pounds, was standing between my knees and about to bite a second time, perhaps maul me. She came running, screaming and shouting and chased him away long enough for me to turn and run away with her. She saved my hands if not my life.

Don't discount her and never underestimate her. She did it... and she won.

She likes to think like that, as if thinking, "I chose right... and I won."

And she did. She won.

Chapter Twelve

Things

Is there an object you pick up and hold it and that
possession reminds you of the one who owned it? Or a thing with a
story and the story follows the thing? Pieces and precious goods
with names attached? The provenance of antiques and treasures
and heirlooms and art and even simple adornments and
accoutrements of lives past and lives present. Perhaps just
something that you can pick up and look at and remember a word,
or remember a lesson from history. There is a kind of knowing that
you have that perhaps no one else shares. A shared heritage or a
secret.

We learned about the language of fans somewhere along
the way.

And we learned about seashells in Papua New Guinea.

We brought back some of the Manus Island green snail shells, land snails not seashells, some of the rarest in the world because they came from that single island. Those connected us forever to the stories there, the refugees and fugitives and outcasts, which we did not know about at the time we got the shells, they were just pretty shells.

Our searches for shells did not stop there, we've searched in Destin and Tybee Island and Dauphin Island and Savannah and Virginia Beach and The Outer Banks and Okracoke Island.

Say it with me, "Seashell Shop and Surf Style Store." Say it again faster, "Seashell shop and surf style store. My sister Sally is a thistle sifter. She works at the sea selling seashells at the seashell shop and surf style store when she isn't sifting thistles."

Once upon a time, while the Dutch East India Company plied trade across the seven seas, the Epitonium Scalare, "the Precious Wentletrap" with its white spirals was considered so rare and valuable that one could get you a house, or at least ensure credit, like the aristocratic emblems and value of pearls.

202

Things. Are all women's houses filled with things? Do they all come adorned with lace and embroidery and gold chains and pearls? Will each one correct you and tell you that the Christmas song says "five **gold** rings" not "five golden rings" and care to explain the difference?

Some old things come with old stories.

Some well-known stories are old before they are ever written. It didn't stop Twice Told Tales from being published or the explanatory cards in the museums from being shared or someone from writing down the Odyssey. Some stories are borrowed and some are stolen. Like things, some stories are passed around, inherited, maybe hidden.

Behind me as I write leans Big Granny's Stick, her walking stick. Who was Big Granny? She was Dr. Harris's grandmother, which would make her Karen's great grandmother, and we have carried and protected her walking stick, a branch of hickory with rubber knobs on each end, across many states through many moves for many years. A stick. Does it have any special story or significance? Yeah, it belonged to Big Granny.

We have Granny Harris's cauldron, a black cast iron pot on short pin "feet" that must be more than a hundred years old because Granny was born around 1912, and the cauldron was said to have been the one that her stepmother was using over an outdoor fire when Granny was a toddler, and the stepmother caught fire and ran in a panic, was engulfed in flames and died. That, too, has traveled with us, and yes, it has looked a bit odd on top of the moving boxes, and no we never use it at Halloween, we have a plastic one for that.

In the curio stand in the corner is a statue that we think is The Hunchback of Notre Dame that came from the antique dealer, Aunt Annie Lee (pronounced "Ant Annuhlee"), and the statue is said to resemble her. That seems a bit harsh and probably untrue, it's probably an exaggeration caused by comparison with her two lovely sisters, one of whom was Grandma Blake whose sepia portrait Karen resembles in uncanny ways.

204

Karen's grandmothers were part of her life until she was nearly 40. She stayed at their houses, laughed with them, read with them, and heard their stories. Grandma Blake had the history and genealogy that enabled Karen's mother to be a Daughter of the American Revolution. Grandma studied the gospels and filled books with scholarly notes of her research on them. No one knows why Grandma never published them.

Granny Harris considered it her duty to know everyone's business and to express plenty of opinions about it. She also considered it her obligation to go through the local cemeteries and replace the old dead flowers with live ones. Granny was the first person I met who could cry about long dead loved ones at any given moment, "I miss her so much," even in the kitchen while reheating leftovers.

Once, on the telephone, she forgot who it was that she was calling and let loose a long string of gossip and opinions about Dr. Harris only to hear, "That's very interesting, mother; this is me."

My mother could be somewhat the same way. I will never know what she said to others but I know some of the things she told siblings and I remember quite a bit of what she said to me. There was never any lack of opinions.

Estha Newman Cook was one of five sisters from Hazlehurst, Mississippi. I've never met Beth Henley (I don't think I have) but I swear she either heard about my mother and aunts or spied on them because Crimes of the Heart bears startling resemblance to our family. So does Arsenic and Old Lace – and my mother used to say so, too! My aunts were characters. One was always telling me about Edgar Cayce and such and I have a wealth of lore dating back to Ur and the ancient Chaldeans from sitting beside Aunt Dorothy ("Dot") on many a hot afternoon (she was the first person with air conditioning in her house... and a color TV). My Aunt Adrienne, the namesake of my youngest child, was my favorite, but she was always aloof and severe. Two ounces of soda pop, no more, no less, and don't ask for a cookie. I didn't really know Myra much. She seemed to come from William Faulkner's world or Flannery O'Connor's, not by anything she said, but to hear the stories told of the Depression and the war and Mississippi in either its pre-war or post-war past. And there was Aunt Lois, who lived "out in the country". If I could only be as healthy and warm as Aunt Lois and live as long! She taught me to like fig preserves and to watch out for ticks. There were no antebellum mansions among them nor old plantations. The term "antebellum" means "pre-war". We often referred to Jackson as "post war", you just had to figure out which war.

In my thirties, a father of four children, I found myself between my mother weeping and my aunt Adrienne crying. "Oh, David, oh, David, it's us, it's us," they cried and wailed. What was us? What was us? They had been watching cable news and saw a story of a toddler torn between two couples, the one that had given the child up for adoption and the one that had raised it and bonded with it until now it was three years old. The whole nation was weeping. I cried, too, as if I had to let go of my own child – but they were weeping because my mother had given me away to my aunt Adrienne as an infant and then two years later took me back, and I went from being a fat and healthy and happy toddler to nearly dying.

Oh, there was so much guilt and remorse! Oh, you just don't know the guilt and remorse!

And they tell me that story in my late thirties? Would they have ever told me if not for TV?

I never knew my grandmothers. My mother was orphaned when she was only eight years old. My Newman grandparents were gone long before I was even born much less knew the word "grandparent". Granny Cook's name was Sammy. I am wearing her wedding ring. I have had it since I was a child and I can hardly believe that I didn't lose it. I used to wear it on my little finger and that was a good thing, too, because it was the only heirloom not stolen when thieves robbed our house on Monroe Street. Granny Cook died when I was two. I have no memories.

Karen has lots of memories, and things to remember them by.

She has her mother's wedding ring. Her mother died when she was in college. She doesn't wear it as her wedding ring, we bought her an antique engagement ring and wedding band for those. Somehow antiques are better than new things. She and I have walked through enough antique malls and flea markets to circumnavigate the globe on foot.

And do I dare to tell about General Beauregard's tea set?

A tea set seems like such a genteel thing.

Karen loves the story about Sammy Cook's father, that's Granny Cook's father, that's my great grandfather, Samuel B. Cook, who was in the Confederate cavalry in "the wahwuh" (in the south, you see, there are diphthongs, there are no single syllable words; but don't say multisyllabic words or people will think you are pretentious and suspect that you are not from around here, that you are lying about being from Mississippi and may even be a spy infiltrating Alabama).

This story comes from J.G. Deupree's account of the Noxubee Squadron of the First Mississippi Cavalry. My great grandfather is in that book about his brigade. No one here agrees with Deupree or anyone else's sentiments about their past cause, but even in the most terrible of wars there can be elegant and pleasant moments like the one he describes from early 1865, the final year of that war.

"The Noxubee Squadron of Pinson's regiment were furloughed for twenty days. It goes without saying, we had the time of our lives. All the delights of home were experienced. I cannot describe them as they deserve to be portrayed, and shall not undertake to do so. But I hazard naught when I claim that Lieutenant S. B. Day," (my great grandfather) "Alec McCaskill, and J.G. Deupree were at least somewhat more fortunate than the others.

"We were challenged one afternoon by three beautiful and amiable and expert chess amateurs, Misses Duck Foote, daughter of our first Captain, Judge H.W. Foote, Patti Lyle, afterwards famous as Mrs. Patti Lyle Collins of the Dead Letter Office in Washington, and Fannie Lucas, afterwards Mrs. Featherstone of Brooksville, to play a consultation game of Chess that evening at the hospitable home of Judge Foote. In the exuberance of joy, we accepted, knowing full well the great pleasure in store for us."

The denouement of that story is that the ladies had a strategy to prevent the cavalry from winning checkmate.

"But, foreseeing this impending disaster, the ladies executed a novel strategy to prevent it. By the tintinnabulation of a tiny bell, they summoned a maid servant bearing a waiter, which contained seven foaming glasses of egg nog, better far, from a soldier's view-point, than the nectar of Olympian Jupiter. The ladies sipped gently while the soldiers drained their glasses. While there is no positive proof that these last glasses were extra-strong, it is certain that an instantaneous thrill sped along the nerves of the cavalrymen, obfuscated their reasoning facilities, and kindled their imaginations. Caring naught for hazard or peril, they shoved the passed pawn, and, forgetting their decision to claim a knight, they called for a queen, which did not check, as the knight would have done. This was fatal. The ladies then quietly pushed forward their passed pawn and very properly claimed a queen, which checked our king and after a few moves affected a mate."

The ladies got them flustered (inebriated?) and beat them. The ladies beat the cavalry.

Aunt Annie Lee, Aunt Fleta Grace's mother and sister to Grandma Blake was with Grandma Blake in New Orleans during The Great Depression when many formerly grand houses of New Orleans sold off their treasures. One such grand house had been the property of General P.T. Beauregard himself and Grandma Blake obtained General Beauregard's tea set, of which Aunt Annie Lee, a bona fide antique appraiser, validated and documented the provenance of said tea set.

Not entirely informed by that typed provenance, I looked up the maker's mark and it is indeed a delicate set from the 1700's made in England or France, of the type frequently sold by merchants in New Orleans in the early 1800's and was very likely from General Beauregard's own family possessions. General Beauregard's tea set.

Karen loves tea sets.

There is a pewter tea set with Chinese dragons that is one of her old favorites, its dark red body with pewter dragons a kind of commanding and beckoning presence on the shelf. She treasures it because she and her father selected it together. They shared a fascination for it when they found it among Aunt Annie Lee's antiques when Karen was thirteen.

Julianne loves tea sets, too, uses and washes and "cures" her tea sets, as if ceremonially cleansing and preserving them.

Tea sets and tankards and china and coffee mugs.

Oh, Lordy, have we got coffee mugs! We have coffee mugs to the point where they tumble from the cabinet! The girls say, "No more coffee mugs! Absolutely no more coffee mugs!" But every week and every trip they bring two home. Just the other day, Miss Don't You Dare Buy Another Coffee Mug brought home a Halloween themed bright orange mug she found in a neighborhood yard sale.

Chapter Thirteen

Out of Time

Karen always wanted a certain kind of silver cross and she was in London where she might find one, desperately wanting the right one before she left; due to everyone putting her off and misdirecting their trip she was running out of time. She was running out of patience, too. On their last day in London the adults in the group kept making decisions about where to go and what to do and a fifteen year old girl, not even one of their own children, hardly had a say in the choosing.

She knew there could be disappointment; she had already experienced several, the worst one was missing out on Stonehenge. The adults had poo-pooed a trip to Stonehenge, even citing religious reasons against going there. Mrs. Aurochs, one of the mothers in the party, said that she wouldn't be caught dead visiting there.

"I read once that Druids sacrificed babies for witches. Who knows what kind of spirits own that place. It's dangerous to tamper with such things."

"It would be vampires that want blood not witches, mother," interjected her son, Jerry.

"I hear what you're saying, Edna, like tarot cards and Ouija boards," agreed Mrs. Ross, leader of the group. "I seem to recall reading the same thing about Stonehenge in the British Museum, and they should know."

Karen was appalled at that, and thought it unlike Mrs. Ross, a seasoned world traveler and educated woman, to defer from visiting such an iconic site on such a lame excuse as fear or distaste of witches and Druids. Perhaps Richard Halliburton never visited it, but she wanted to go there, and even if it wasn't one of The Seven Wonders of the World, Karen would put it on a short list of places to see in England. Besides, if you're avoiding Druids, there goes France, and if you can't walk in the haunts of witches there goes more than half of the British Isles. It was the kind of thing that kept stalling her trip, putting her off, derailing her expectations.

Mrs. Ross was Karen's piano teacher and had organized the tour, comprised of two or three families of Aurochs and Kleinets, their teenage children and some grandchildren. Karen was the lone Harris, invited to join because she was Mrs. Ross's dear friend and favorite pupil – and because Mrs. Ross could tell that Karen was knowledgeable and had good judgments about things to see and do, and she knew that Karen would be a good companion for talking.

London in June 1974 was raining and cool, an unexpected contrast to the rest of their summery touring through Italy and France.

"I suppose that rain in London is to be expected," said Mrs. Ross, resigned to fate.

"It's easy to imagine London in winter," said Karen. "I like winter."

"You look like you dressed for it, too," said Mrs. Kleinet. "Isn't that long sleeve knit turtleneck a bit hot?"

Karen looked at the sleeve of her brown and white striped shirt. It seemed to her that she blended right in with the styles and colors around them. "It isn't hot today."

"I suppose not," agreed Mrs. Ross, "especially since it's raining. It's been raining the whole time we've been here, all three days." She sighed.

Small talk and shopping, was it always weather, small talk and shopping, and long discussions about where to eat? Trying to quibble over prices and salads took as much time as actually eating.

The rain made it seem oddly dark and black for summer. The trees were black and their leaves were black, too. The rain sometimes slowed them down as they visited cathedrals and museums, shopping, dining, and always quibbling. Not everything

218

was agreeable to the others in their tour. "I wonder what we should do?"

"I wonder if they can ever clean the sooty grime from these old buildings," Mrs. Aurochs said.

"It's kind of Dickensian, don't you think?" Karen said, "Like tarnished silver."

"Sterling silver, of course," said Mrs. Ross, smiling at her own cleverness. "I noticed that you passed up a lot of things that were silver, Karen"

"They were silver plate. Silver plate doesn't have lasting value. The silver wears off, then what do you have? But real silver always keeps its value, even when it tarnishes; you can clean the tarnish away."

Talk of silver just kept her mind on her quest, and made her gnaw her lip as she watched time slip away. Her anxiety and anticipation was getting desperate, but she was part of a group, a younger part of a group, not even related by family to anyone in the group. Nothing could elevate Karen's right to vote on where to go and what to do.

The whole group was going to end the day – and the trip – in Harrods. Karen was beside herself wishing to escape and find at least one thing she had wanted, hopefully a silver one, one with some meaning and connection, not just a tourist trinket one could buy anywhere. She had passed up plenty of plain ones in gift shops, at cathedrals and museums, in shop windows on the streets, in hopes that one unique meaningful object waited for her to make her trip memorable and complete. She told this to Mrs. Ross who said she understood and promised to go with Karen to find one before they boarded the bus to Heathrow in late afternoon to depart.

"But I can't let you go off alone," Mrs. Ross said.

Karen believed that she would be perfectly fine alone, and actually felt like she might be more capable than Mrs. Ross or any of the other ladies, at finding her own way and taking care of herself. She'd managed alone many times. Her father and brother could tell you.

"Well, 'England swings', you know, as they say, and a pretty American teenage girl has no business wandering the streets by herself."

Karen was fifteen, about to turn sixteen in September, determined to start college at sixteen. She had completed her junior year of high school, got special permission to graduate early, and as far as she was concerned the tour of Europe with Mrs. Ross was her "senior trip".

The streets were filled with young men, Karen noticed, even in the rain. Some of them seemed very hairy and she didn't care for that. Men with bushy long hair and bell bottom jeans, gold chains around their necks and wrists. Lanky long legged young men standing in doorways shielded from the rain smoking. Benson and Hedges ads – longer and with Special Filters – were everywhere in the Underground and the Marlboro Man in his sheepskin jacket seemed weirdly out of place in England. Some of the smoke smelled good. Occasionally she thought she whiffed the fragrance of vanilla. Too many men had long hair, she thought. The wet weather seemed to add body to her own long hair, which she really didn't want or need. She looked around and thought that everyone had lots of hair, sometimes big hair and bouncy hair, and maybe a bit too much facial hair. Heavy mustaches were in fashion and she thought some of the ones that grew down to the chin looked odd without a beard. Many had sideburns and mustaches, but not many beards.

When they were on the street outside Harrods, Karen and Mrs. Ross, another teenage girl from the group, Martha, stopped outside the doors gazing up, taking pictures of the flags that lined the roof of the colossal store.

"I can see the red maple leaf of Canada's flag, but I can't see the American one," Martha said pointing her camera up and shooting. It wasn't raining much, just intermittent drops.

Karen had taken plenty of pictures, too, but at the late hour of their final day felt exasperation at yet another delay, tensely realizing at the same time that she needed to be patient and polite with her companion. A rebuke from Mrs. Ross or one of the mothers might mean another delay or even a disaster.

A young man passed by them, brushing close to Karen, wearing a navy blue pea coat, his collar turned up beside his cheeks, and she thought, "My, it really is the wrong season for that." All the same, she thought his prominent nose was attractive and his face seemed determined and intelligent. He was walking swiftly and purposefully, as if he knew precisely where he was going and what he would do once he got there, and she thought she could someday fall in love with a man like that. But... only hurry... time waits for no man, and the last day was quickly fading.

"Come on inside for now," Karen told Martha. "You'll get your camera wet."

Mrs. Ross was standing just inside the entrance of Harrods, looking around, sometimes standing on tiptoe, leaning above other's shoulders, and craning her neck to see over the tourists crowding into the store. "Do you see Mrs. Aurochs and Mrs. Kleinet? They said they'd be here, and we're already a bit late."

At precisely that moment, Mrs. Aurochs walked in, shaking her new Burberry, and apologized, "I stopped in Chinacraft across the street. Couldn't help myself. I want to take it all home."

Karen tried imagining that. She wasn't all that impressed by Chinacraft when she passed by the store, but she did notice the sets of genuine silverware. The patterns looked antique. The notion of steamer trunks and boarded crates and chains presented an image that she quickly brushed aside.

Karen had been told for days not to worry, putting her off, because she was bound to find anything she wanted in Harrods. Mrs. Ross said to Karen, "I'm sure that you'll find what you want in here. It has the reputation that you can find anything you want in the world here. Things from all over the world." A big store, and it seemed crowded.

Mrs. Ross was round and stout, "not to be messed with,"

Karen would say. She looked nice but nondescript. She might have

been taller, once, but seemed like average height beside Karen. Her

beakish nose meant business and no nonsense. Other people

thought that Mrs. Ross was stern but she was always nice to Karen,

and to Karen Mrs. Ross was her favorite teacher. Karen felt very

grateful for being able to go along on the trip. Karen had been

chastised twice already, early on in the journey, not individually

herself for her own behavior, but as one of the teenagers in the

group. She felt that was unfair, the worst suffering of all, an

undeserved admonishment just because she was a teen and a girl

and with the bunch.

Karen knew that she could get through the biggest places in

surprisingly short time, and a filled and crowded place like Harrods

seemed daunting and tiring, overstuffed, all wrong and only put her

off more. After an hour of concentrated searching, especially amid

the jewelry, Karen told Mrs. Ross that she was done with Harrods, and conveyed how anxious she was to find what she was looking for and how concerned she was that time was running out.

"Well, if it's not in here after all it's in London," Mrs. Ross said. "There are plenty of shops along the street. We'll find something, and I promised I would go. Come along."

With minutes ticking swiftly away, they bustled out of the massive store, away from the crowd and onto the rain-washed street.

The visual impression even at midday was black and brown. Karen looked backward at "HARRODS" in capital serif letters down a corner of the store. The flags of nations waved colorfully above, not limp or bedraggled despite the rain. She felt urgency, not panic and not disillusionment. She knew what she wanted and she felt that if she was allowed freedom to search for it she would find it. As they hurried away from Harrods she felt at the end, after all that long trip, that she was free.

Karen almost bumped into a young man in front of them as he pulled a pocket watch on a chain out of his jeans pocket and Karen was surprised by the sight of a pocket watch which seemed Victorian and antique, thinking a wristwatch would be much more practical, just as they passed a jewelry shop window crowded with Omega watches. She thought, who needs a in a city with so many clocks? She saw sweeping second hands wipe the time off all the synchronized watches in the window. Clocks were everywhere, on corners, on shops, and they could hear the chimes of Big Ben. Was London about anything other than time and obsessed with keeping time? At that moment she was obsessed with time. Only hurry, she repeated to herself. At that moment, she was the one obsessed with time. She was with her piano teacher, but the only music came from horns and tires and motor engines, and incessant ticking clocks.

"We don't need to waste time going down a rabbit hole," said Mrs. Ross. "I suppose it's a bit like hide and seek."

Karen did not appreciate the comparison at that moment, and Knightsbridge felt a long way from Wonderland, but she had a quick comeback. "It's more like a scavenger hunt, really, one where I have to find the right cross. A scavenger hunt with a short list."

"Well, I suppose it's a finite task," Mrs. Ross said, "and even though it's a challenge with an uncertain outcome, it can't occupy us that long."

A tall balding man chasing a yellow cocker spaniel as he shouted at it to stop, ran across the sidewalk in front of them chasing the dog across the street and stumbled over the opposite curb disappearing behind a hedge. His pants legs were darkly soaked to the knees.

Karen looked at her own shoes which weren't all that wet, but since they were loafers her socks might be getting damp. She didn't really care. Keep moving. She thought her loafers were fine for all the walking they did. Pull-on brown loafers not penny loafers, she hated those. Just keep moving.

Five girls with red hair, all similarly dressed, crossed the street together, talking and laughing, all enjoying each other's company. As they passed in front of her, blindly causing her and Mrs. Ross to abruptly stop their headlong dash, Karen noticed that one of them was clutching her necklace, a silver necklace, and one of her companions seemed to be watching that, too.

"Excuse me," Karen said on impulse, "I couldn't help noticing your necklace. Where did you get it?"

Now that they were stopped, Karen thought the girls looked like sisters of varying ages younger than her. They smiled and seemed calmly helpful and attentive.

"I got it just down the street, actually, just now, at the train station."

The other girls nodded in agreement, as if accentuating "That's right" and watched Karen who merely replied, "Thank you" and seemed intent to move on, so the five redheaded girls continued their way and Karen with Mrs. Ross barreled onward, but now with purpose.

"Train station?" Mrs. Ross puzzled. "Train station? You don't suppose she meant Victoria station, do you? That means we better hurry."

A teenage boy with red hair sat under a pub umbrella thoughtfully writing in a journal, sometimes pressing his pen to his lips; he occasionally seemed to be reciting some line to himself, and looking pleased, writing it down. The sight made Karen curious about what he was writing. An Indian man, possibly in his young thirties, was bouncing a toddler boy up and down while they waited, sheltered by an awning, waiting for a shopper who must be inside. The red phone boxes caught her eye, smokers leaning against them even though it was raining.

Train station, down the street; train station, her mind kept repeating. Keep moving. Hurry.

She didn't even realize how fast they were going, passing shop after shop, but never one that looked like the right one, not wandering into any shops, not even browsing in windows, just walking fast as if they had a singular purpose and destination, and were surprised to find themselves at Knightsbridge tube station. Karen was startled that they had gotten down the street so fast and not entered so much as one shop, but her mind kept repeating "train station".

The tube station?

"We're at the underground," Karen said. "Do you suppose she meant the tube train?"

"Let's try down there," suggested Mrs. Ross. "It will get us out of the rain."

Try? Try? Karen felt a certainty. This was the place, she just knew it.

The curb and steps seemed dirty and black, but all the tube stations seemed that way. They made your shoes and socks and cuffs and hems dirty and black after a day about town in London, getting on and off buses and trains; that was a price you paid, touring London, getting grimy with black at the ends. At the end of the underground stairs, in a corner before the turnstiles, was a small shop tucked away like a cupboard in that corner, and Karen immediately saw a case of jewelry and felt certain that what she had been seeking was there. The sounds and smells of the underground slipped away like background noise as she concentrated her attention on the items in that single display case.

A little silver replica of St. Martin's Cross from Iona. Karen recognized it as soon as she saw it.

"That's an antique, that is, turn of the century, genuine silver," said the shopkeeper. "Go ahead and pick it up; it has images on both sides. I think that's very unusual, not something you can find just any place. I don't think they'd have that even at Harrods."

Karen held it in her hand, examining it. A little silver cross, not polished or shiny, looking every bit of seventy or eighty years, maybe older. It was indeed different than all the others she had seen, not decorated on one side only to be flat on the other; it was like a little silver replica of the real historic cross on the island of Iona, with Bible characters and scenes on both sides. Balls in cross patterns and never-ending Celtic designs on one side, Christ enthroned flanked by the bull of St. Luke and the lion of St. Mark. Was that Daniel among lions or an early Christian martyr? Was that Jesus being arrested by the Romans? Were those the women who went to the tomb? Were the four the four evangelists, the writers of the gospels? Finely and intricately detailed. Genuine silver.

"Yes, this is exactly what I want."

Karen had a fascination for Celtic crosses since childhood and she wanted to obtain one. Her grandmother had one, a rather large ornate silver cross, which was beautiful, but far too large and ornate for Karen. She had grown up a Presbyterian, and she saw Scottish crosses every Sunday at church. As a teenager, she often drew the outlines of a Celtic cross as a doodle, especially on church bulletins during the service. And on that June day in London she finally had the one she wanted, the one that suited her.

233

"I understand what it's like to want just the right thing," said Mrs. Ross, "to appreciate and want a fine thing. After all, I kept the big marble bar from the Ross Building when they tore it down." That was true, and she put it in the living room of her very old house on Pine Street in the old part of Hattiesburg, Mississippi.

"I'll put it on a chain I have at home, when I get back," Karen said, and the seller put it in a little box.

The touring party was still touring Harrods when they rejoined them.

"Let's ride taxis back to the hotel; they have such a London charm."

Robert and Martha joined Karen and Mrs. Ross in a cab.

Looking out the cab window Karen said, "I love history. I love thinking about all the poets and authors. It seems like every story I know came from here. It's like they all lived and died here."

"They're probably buried here, too, in the walls somewhere like Westminster Abbey," Robert, Martha's older brother said.

A gray image of Poets Corner spread across Karen's memory like a backdrop or a screen she could examine later. At that moment in the London cab on her way to the hotel to board a bus taking her to her plane to go home she had in her pocket a little white box with a silver cross, the one that she wanted, the one she had been looking for, the one she knew she would find with the same certainty she recognized the place.

Chapter Fourteen

Conversations

I walk into the bookstore. Well, this is different, the oak doors are electric and open inward on their own. They weren't like that. When did they change this?

There's no one here, not at the kiosk or over at the magazines. I don't see anyone. The escalator is working, I'll go up to the café. I still don't see anyone. I turn past the tables of books, the shelves of new ones and I see Karen still sitting where she was the other day, with her iPhone.

"There must be some way out of here," I say as I sit down.

She looks up. "Not until you get that book."

"I got it, the other day while we were here. I'm working on this one now. I feel like I'm reading this while I write it; it's just pouring out like that."

She looks like she's thinking about that, and then looks down at her phone.

"What are you looking at?"

She laughs and smiles. "It's that video of the baby waving bye-bye to the turtle in the lily pond. It's just so cute."

"Is that on Instagram?"

"WhatsApp, she uses WhatsApp. Do you want to see it?"

"I saw it. I love the photos, too. You sent them to me." Her Fit Bit is on one wrist and her Apple Watch is on the other.

"Did you go for a walk?" I ask.

She makes a face. "I haven't gotten five thousand steps yet today. Want to go for a walk together?"

"I suppose we could walk around the mall."

Her mouth tilts. "I hate that. You know I don't like walking around the mall. And they put the decorations up too soon. It's way too early."

"I don't know; I kind of need the decorations right now. I'd like for it to be Christmas."

She's in a black pullover sweater with a white button shirt underneath. Isn't that an outfit she used to have, years ago?

"You know, just when I really like your hair and I tell you how much I like it you cut it short."

"I like it short," she says and looks at her phone.

"I got stuck on the chapter about graduate school. I had written three thousand words but I hated them. I just thought it was boring. I don't want something to be boring and pedantic."

Her mouth straightens out.

"What do I think of when I think of grad school at JMU? I think of putting those three years to use as best as possible to advance myself to where I wanted to go, the jobs I took on that did that, those were the things I wanted to work in, so I was publicist for the art department, and I managed the opera theatre. Those things moved me along to where I wanted to go."

"That's a better way to say it than what I was writing, but that's too brief, only seventy-eight words. It needed more than that, and I kept writing about me. I'm not here to write about me."

She bunches up her mouth as if she understands that.

"I don't know what to say about Kansas, either. I'm not really trying to write a travelogue or a history, I'm trying to tell about you as a person. I reckoned you'd like a chapter about the mountains and hiking, that it would say things you'd like."

She smiles at that, a really pleased smile.

But now I find myself in Kansas. I mean, I am outside the old hospital that had been turned into the college art department where I worked. I guess I'll go to my office. The outside door is not electric. Of course it's not. What would change here? Nothing.

Nothing changes here. The panic bar seems like it's on the wrong side, wrong way around, but I push it and I'm in.

"Joe?" I call out. He's not here. All the lights are on and my door is open. Of course it's open, it's always open.

The pampas grass is drumming at the window and the wind begins to howl.

There is no one in my office. Of course there isn't. My old wooden desk is such an embarrassment, all beat up and so small. I think it must have come out of an old dorm. There is no way to know how old it is. But it sure does resonate sound well. When my music plays on my computer it sounds really good.

Where is Karen?

Here she is, at my door.

"There's nothing in the gallery right now."

"We're between shows. I don't have a budget for frames, so all I can do is wait for The Prairie Art Show to start or put up one of the old shows. The college probably expects for me to pony up out of my own pocket and pay for frames."

"It's nice to keep the shows going, keep something up there. If you don't, I'm afraid Education will take that space. You don't want it to look as if you don't care."

She grabs a stool that someone left in the hall and pulls it into the office. There isn't much space. It must have been an office when it was a hospital, there isn't enough space for it to have been an examining room. Everyone who comes in is knee-to-knee and nose-to-nose.

"Did I ever tell you that I think I met a ghost here once?"

She looks impatient with that. "You know I don't believe in that sort of thing." Then she smiles. "But you know I love to hear a story and I like spooky stories."

"This one isn't spooky. He was wearing a flannel shirt and he said he built the hospital. But he couldn't have even been sixty years old and this place was built fifty-five years before. He toured

241

me around where the x-ray machine had been and told me about people who died here."

The pampas grass is still beating on the window and the wind is whistling now.

"I really can't stay here long."

"Me, neither," I say. "I hear my pulse thrumming in my ears."

"I really think you should see a doctor. When was the last time you had a check-up?"

"Karen, he checked me out when I went in for the dog bite."

"That's not a check-up! That's not a full physical. At your age you should be going in and getting a full physical."

"You still need to see a counselor," I say. "You go see the anger management counselor first, and then I'll go for a physical."

"We aren't bargaining here," she says.

"Where is here?" I ask. "It doesn't seem like my office anymore. In fact, it really looks like a cloisters, like the cloisters in Iona."

The sun is brightly lighting the inner courtyard but the colonnaded path is shaded.

"Did you get to look through the shop to see if they had another cross?"

"Yes, but I didn't see one. The old one was an antique when I got it, and that was in London. It was silver."

"I've been leaving you alone and letting you wander on your own. I didn't know how you were feeling here. I know that you've wanted to come here for a long time."

We're walking between sunlight and shadow here, amid the low carved arches.

"Did you tell your friend that we're coming to England?"

"No, I just wanted it to be you and me, so we can talk."

"Some people think that we talk to each other plenty. Some even say we talk too much."

"There's never too much," she says. "And we like to see the same things and go to the same places."

"That's how we always knew we were friends."

"Why are you just circling around this part?" she asks.

"I love a cloister. There's a part of one inside the Nelson-Adkins, and you know how much I love The Cloisters in New York. How will we get to Chillingborn in Kent?"

"There isn't a Chillingborn, don't be silly. I told you about the Kent railway. I have it all figured out. I don't even think we need a car."

"You want to walk the Pilgrim Trail to Canterbury, don't you?"

"Oh, yes, yes, I do!" And she's holding my arm.

And the columns have become the Georgia pines of the woodland trail.

"The pine straw smells sweet. Why don't we walk here every day? How could I ever move away from this?"

"The pastor search is going well. I really want something I can sink my teeth into. I like to start things and build things," she's saying.

"We don't need to walk any faster," I say. "Three miles per hour is fine. Your body burns fat and converts sugar better at three miles per hour. I don't want to start burning protein."

"How do your pancreas and liver know how to do these things?" She looks at her Apple watch. "No signal. Here we are in the middle of suburbia and no signal."

"It's the dead zone of the park," I say. "This is where your phone calls cut out."

There are some giant orange mushrooms next to a tree at a dark bend of the trail.

"Julianne would hate that, she's terrified of mushrooms," I say. "Should I send her pictures?"

"Don't be awful. That's mean."

"About as mean as tickling your feet, I suppose."

"Don't start talking about tickling."

"I really am stuck in the book. I want it to show you. It's a book about you and it keeps turning into a book about places and things."

"Maybe you can tell the things I like."

"I did some of that, and that is still all about things. If I can't publish it, I'll just give it to you as a present and it can be yours."

"Like the poems."

"Like the poems."

"I want you to paint something for the living room, David, something to go above the mantle in that empty space. I've been asking for that for two years."

246

"I know that. I'm yet a bit inhibited by the lack of working space. I'm trying. There's the lake."

It's windy across the lake, but soundless, the way the wind can be in Georgia. I can see that it's windy but I can't hear it.

"I can't tell the direction sound is coming from anymore," I say.

"Me, too, I've been having problems with that. I think I hear someone from one side of the house but then they're on the other. I suppose we ought to get that checked."

"Well, we do have insurance. I'm hoping something comes through on the dog bite. Does everything that happens have to just cost me and cost me out of my pocket? Can't somebody else pay for a change?"

"Did you talk with Nathan today?" she asks. "We talked for hours today. He has worked through some things and he has some really good insights."

"He always has good insights. He thinks and feels very deeply."

I stop.

She stops and looks at me.

The pine trees. The sky. The green grassy hill topped by towering white clouds in the blue. She made a video of Adrienne running up the hill and spinning around like Maria in The Sound of Music and it looks just like it. We live in a place that can be like that. And it can look like Selznick's Zenda, like the old Ruritanian hunting forest and its streams.

"Want to go to Helen? We can eat at the Old Heidelburg. 'The Old Heidelburg', what a name, what a joke, Sixties and clapboard just to get people to go shopping…"

"I'll go anywhere with you, just so we can be alone in the car and talk."

"You know I've become terrified to think ahead about driving."

She makes a face. "I don't understand that."

"I get scared when I think about driving into Atlanta, when I imagine going to the airport. I'm scared ahead of time, but once I'm on the road and driving I'm okay. Maybe I've driven too much, too many miles, had too many close calls, and I start imagining things and feeling the weight of statistics. There was some guy stopped – just stopped, I guess he was texting – across the double yellow line on my side of Russell Road yesterday. I started honking and he moved on, turned, never even looked up."

"Like that woman in the SUV the other day!" Karen looks freshly pissed. "She just came over, no blinker, nothing, and nearly hit us!"

"Every morning in the dark at the school when I drop off Adrienne, someone has gone around the barricade and they're coming head on. They don't even try to miss me. What really gets me is that every time there is someone doing something seriously wrong they look and act as if they have every right to do it.

"Maybe it all starts to add up and takes over my imagination. But I can't really think about driving anywhere. I just have to know it is coming, say that at this or that hour I have to do it, and then do it. Once I'm in the car and going I'm fine. These days, just lately, I'd rather stay home. I like the house."

Like where we're sitting, right now, in the kitchen at the table.

"Remember the time we were sitting in the old house in Jackson and we thought we heard voices, static buzzing voices like on a bad radio?"

"Oh, I know, that was so creepy!" She put her phone on the table. "What was that quote you put on Facebook the other day?"

"John Donne, Air and Angels: 'Nor in nothing nor in things extreme and scattering bright can love inhere.' It was from a poem."

"What does that mean?"

"For love, it means you can't love nothing, nothing is nothing; you have to love something. Things extreme mean you can't love things that are far-fetched and grandiose, or scattered like the stars. You have to love what's in front of you."

"I wish people could hear you preaching. I wish they could hear the things you say, the things you tell me, how you pull things together. You see things so differently from the way others do. When you start out I'm confused and I don't follow and I wonder where it's going, and then – bam! – you've made your case and I think, ha!, and I want to tell someone else."

"That's the artist," I say opening my laptop, "putting it together, bit by bit."

"You make such good coffee, I wish other people could taste your coffee."

"We should sell cakes," I say, "but then we'd have to admit to what was in them and own up to where we got the recipe. I'd have to do that for my blended coffee."

"You make such good coffee."

"Well, it's a bit late for coffee. I'll bring you some in the morning, like I always do."

Like I always do.

Chapter Fifteen

Pictures

I think I'm writing something brilliant and then I read someone else's social media post with 300 words that are so succinct and insightful that I think, well, crap, that beats all 24,000 words that I've been writing. It's the highest compliment you can give anyone to think goddamn I wish I'd written that, but you didn't.

Maybe pictures are better.

There's a black and white photograph of Karen sitting in a patio chair in Lae painted by the equatorial sun, her legs stretched out with a copy of Vogue magazine spread across her lap. "How cool is that? Reading Vogue in Papua New Guinea." And she looks cool, like she ought to be in Vogue.

I painted a watercolor of her while I was telling her about drybrush and stippling and scumbling in Ukarumpa. She's in a yellow shirt, her head turned toward me. I did it from a photograph of her in the golden hour of the day as the setting sun painted her face on the dirt path home from the school to the missionary house. She looks like a kid in the photograph, her arms full of books, like how could she be so far away from home, it must be summer camp or something, but, no, we were nine thousand miles from home across the Pacific. I must have ruined five number two Windsor Newton brushes on that one little painting, scumbling and scraping the dry color thickly onto the pressed paper until I'd worn all the hairs away. That was when I wanted to be Andrew Wyeth. How many brushes did that man go through? Who has the time like that for egg tempera? Not me, I can't even seem to stop wolfing down my food.

There is a sepia tone photograph of us that we took the first time we went to the State Fair. She was eighteen and she was sick but she didn't want to miss the fair. Her cheeks must have been flushed with fever because her face looks radiant. She chose an antebellum dress that looks better than the Gibson girl (I know, that's much later than antebellum, but she looks better in it than Miss Melanie and not scandalous like Miss Scarlett) so I put on the jacket of a Confederate colonel.

She does look something like Olivia de Havilland but better, somehow gentler, her perfect chin doesn't move into a V the way the actress's did, and her eyes seem calmer and quieter.

There's a picture of her on Little Stony Man cliff in jeans and a hat, as commanding as any shot of Bette Davis skiing, like she's on top of the world with all the valley stretching out three thousand feet below.

I tried to paint her in her wedding dress, but her facial expressions change too fast. A 30 by 40 piece of watercolor paper can seem pretty big, painting from life, with someone sitting in her wedding dress.

We were talking about pictures the other day and Adrienne had never seen pictures of her grandmothers.

Mrs. Harris and her lovely smile, she looked like the epitome of the Fifties ideal. She kept her eyeglasses on for the photograph. She was Phi Mu at Newcomb College in New Orleans; Julianne joined Phi Mu, too, at William & Mary. I can see Karen and Janet and Julianne and Adrienne easily in her face.

My mother was Miss Jackson of 1940 and I have two pictures of her as beauty queen, one in a rose color gown and one in a swimsuit with a ribbon across her torso saying "Miss Jackson 1940".

Adrienne liked the swimsuit picture.

My leggy mother was only five foot three but everyone thought she was tall. Mom often bought "junior" size dresses and shopped in "petit". She seemed like The Strong Irish Woman and the gentle sweet soul like Miss Melanie, patient to a fault, except she wasn't, but she was. She was and she wasn't. I thought she could be anxious and high strung sometimes and had a high and sudden temper, but how do you tell that to others when everyone around you thinks she's an angel of mercy?

Actresses remind me of my mother. They did her, too. She said people compared her to Irene Dunne. I can see that, sort of. Karen compared her to Mary Astor, but I could never see that. Maybe it was an air of nervous anticipation? The two that even now still and always have reminded me of my mother were Maureen O'Hara and Rita Hayworth. My mom seemed like she always wanted to dance. She didn't, she just moved that way. And she was obsessed with shoes. I have never seen anyone with so many shoes. I think I learned the names of colors by shopping with her for shoes. Mauve, taupe, beige, alabaster, crimson, carnation, carnelian, crepe, crinoline, I'm getting lost in this...

Pictures, pictures, everywhere. My mother on a bench in Japan, patiently waiting for Dad to stop giving speeches and taking pictures.

Mom said that she fell in love with Dad because of his smile, and that he looked like Gene Kelly. I never saw that. I never saw any resemblance between my father and Gene Kelly. Sometimes Your Host Walt Disney would remind me of Dad, because of the gray suit, I think, and the square chin, and the air of selling something. Dad may have been a colonel in World War II but I suspect he got there as a salesman. He seemed as if he was always wanting to be a salesman.

My mother on the side of the road, standing in a dark suit, you'd think she was six feet tall, my older sister beside her in pigtails, maybe as young as five, an old Ford with thick steel walls way back behind them.

I painted several watercolors from that one photograph, years ago, when I tried to tell the narrative of their lives through pictures.

I can see my mother and her Newman family in Katy Lynn's face and her black hair. Katy Lynn loves Ireland.

Pictures everywhere of Karen. Adrienne laughs and says, "Mom takes a picture of a tree and Dad is taking a picture of Mom while she takes a picture of the tree."

I used to take pictures of her every time she turned her head, the way her face would catch the light, the changes in her hazel eyes.

There she is, there she is, there she is...

In a coat on the deck of the Constitution in Boston.

In a sun dress on the deck of the Constellation in Baltimore.

In that green sun dress in Papua New Guinea.

In her gray coat with the collar pulled up to her face in the old wingback chair with the shepherds print.

At The Ruins of Windsor.

At the Valentine banquet in Papua New Guinea in that fantastic blue-violet dress.

Crossing the Thames at Westminster Bridge.

Crossing the Millennium Bridge.

Carving a pumpkin, in a striped sailor shirt.

With the kittens asleep across her neck.

Curled up with a book in the window.

There she is, there she is, there she is...

There she is with a black line under her mouth where she almost bit through her own lip during labor.

There she is through a Leica.

There she is beside the lake through a Nikon.

There she is in India through an iPhone 5.

What about a black-and-white through a green filter?

What if I use a red filter so the clouds look great and the blue sky looks black? No, that will make your face too white.

How about a polarizing filter?

How about a telephoto? Those are great for portraits. I want a 90mm lens for this Leica. Perhaps for Christmas?

Okay, now I have the Olympus e-PL1... how do I change the shutter speeds? I can't wait around for the smartphone to decide when to take the picture. I can't previsualize and anticipate the moment that way. Oh, look, here's how I change it... ISO 3200 and 1/2000 of a second and I caught the hummingbird. Yay! Look! That can be my wallpaper.

She's not the only girl in the house.

There she is Sarah Lambert with green bead earrings next to her red hair.

There she is three year old Anna Lara with her mouth open and her hands up as if she'll either eat the world or shout it down.

There's Anna Lara in black-and-white in her mother's arms at the National Zoo, the Washington Zoo.

And there are Sarah Lambert and Anna Lara at Anna Lara's American wedding recreating the photo of them when they were six and three.

Julianne dressed up as Zorro.

Julianne thrusting a sabre and winning second place at her freshman fencing tournament.

Katy Lynn on another movie set. Look! She's in the trailer! How many times is she in the trailer? Did you find yourself in the movie? Yay! She's in the movie! We counted four times!

There she is and there she is and there she is and there she is...

There is Julianne in the playground looking as if she is in charge.

There's Katy Lynn beside the lake at the Dillon Nature Center in Kansas. She looks so thoughtful.

There's Adrienne with her Second Place prize in the county Science Fair.

There's Adrienne with Charlie in the photo booth at Homecoming.

And here is a photograph of Nathan, one he likes, in a green frame wearing all of the Green Lantern rings, pointing his fist up at me to show them off or to shoot power.

And here he is, under the old tulip poplar tree, the tallest tree in Bridgewater, hugging his sisters, sweet and loving with love to spare.

And the young man, lifting Katy Lynn up in triumph after her graduation.

And in make-up after How to Succeed in Business, holding his little sister Adrienne in his arms and carrying her around among the other actors backstage.

Sarah Lambert and Jordan on stage... was that 1940's Radio Hour? Or was that Babes in Arms? Is Jordan sticking his tongue in her ear?

There in the brilliant sun under the vast sky of India, Vashisht throwing yellow petals joyously into the air on the day after their wedding.

We have our wedding pictures. There we are hugging after the reception, with me in that brown suit stupidly forgetting my wallet was still in the tuxedo.

Chapter Sixteen

The Elephant

She walked into the music building and asked where she could find a practice room.

It was a late summer day, if there ever is such a thing as late summer in Mississippi where the summers seem to never end until they take a hard slap from winter or have cold water dumped on them in autumn. I was standing in the shadows of the lobby talking to my girlfriend, Denise, not succeeding at getting her to agree to go with me to dinner later, when Karen walked in looking as if she expected something to be prepared for her and puzzled that she didn't find it waiting.

"Where can I find a practice room, one with a piano?"

I told her that they were downstairs.

Whoever wrote that script loved contrasts because Karen seemed like a high school kid in the wrong space or a doll dressed in an outfit belonging to medieval madrigals. Her long hair was like an emblem of protection or for security of some kind, or an ornament that represented her good upbringing. She was not quite pre-Raphaelite Ophelia. Good middle class family seemed to follow her like an invisible banner.

After she walked past and went downstairs, my other friend, Denise said, somewhat icily, "She looks like a doll." And I remember her studying me, perhaps scrutinizing my demeanor. "Do you think she's a student? She looks too young," she added.

I was just standing there, my head oddly tilted to the side. Somehow I felt that I was in the wrong place and I didn't know what time it was, as if I may have missed an appointment but I wasn't sure where.

"I can see that you remembered something you have to do," Denise said.

Not even coming quite back to where I had been I think I just said, "Bye" or something like that, and left.

It was my second year at college. I had been accepted into choir, which caused quite an upset in the art program because they felt I was being disloyal to visual art by hobnobbing in music, and a stir among some of the young women who wondered if it was an ulterior move on my part to chase them. It was really my effort to do what many of my other efforts were for, to overcome fear. I just hated to admit that I was afraid of the choir director and afraid to sing in public. If someone thought I was trying to do something for my ego they were right but what they didn't know was that I was constantly hoping to salvage it.

The choir director scared me to death. He scared a lot of people. I had asked to join the choir to prove to myself that I was not afraid to talk to him. Mr. Henry Thomas Ford had been a Marine sergeant in Corregidor in World War II and stood six feet four inches with black hair and occasionally arching brows that appeared as though he disapproved of something. Maybe he just disapproved of having to look at you while you were in his way. He was tall but he wasn't standing anymore, he was in a wheelchair.

I can't remember when I became his driver, maybe it was before I met Karen, at the start of that September or perhaps later in the year. Sitting here thinking about it I guess I had sort of encamped in Music, taking piano lessons, practicing at all hours through the night, taking voice lessons, joining the choir, driving the choir director, pulling his wheelchair with him in it up and down stairs, and spending time with him to eat dinner. I think my mother was a bit confused by it, too.

"Are you in music or in art? I thought you started there in English and that you were going to be a reporter. These people aren't going to take care of you, you know." I will protect my mother's sainted memory and not tell the other things she said.

Mr. Ford and I often ate at Primos Restaurant on North State Street near the old Baptist Hospital. Primos Restaurant looked like a throwback even in the Seventies, as if it belonged in the Forties. Humphrey Bogart would have blended right in there.

They had the greatest pastries, in a glass case in front, brownies with powdered sugar, just enough of it and never too much, frosted over them. White table cloths, white Naugahyde booths, the impression was like an old movie with a big band and Cab Calloway, except that Cab Calloway and the orchestra must have left for downtown. In those years I think I lived in a Humphrey Bogart fantasy. Here's looking at you, kid.

Karen joined the choir, but she belonged there. She actually had musical knowledge and musical talent. She arrived able to play Chopin nocturnes. I had started piano lessons for the very first time a year before, learning what a quarter note was and practicing every night just to hack my way through "Go Tell Aunt Rhody".

When did she and I first talk? It was just before Christmas, after she was done with final exams but she hadn't gone home. I had walked into her dorm which was also my girlfriend's dorm, looking for a trail of the girl I was chasing, and there was Karen reading poetry. We struck up a conversation about poetry. At some point she said that she wrote some and I said that I did, too. So I

269

agreed to go home and get mine and she went upstairs and got hers. After I came back, only a few minutes later, we talked and talked about writing poetry.

We did not go out on a date until the next semester, in January of 1977.

"I see that you're spending a lot of time with Karen," my former girlfriend said. "How's that going?"

"She likes me. She's very smart; you should trust her opinions."

We went everywhere together. Sledding when it snowed – we had the magical experience of a rare Mississippi snow together. We walked to the old soda fountain. We walked around the lake and talked. She watched me paint. We were in the piano rooms at the same time. Until May 1977 and it had to come to an end.

I don't remember now how we parted for summer, what understandings we had between us.

We wrote letters. She said I wrote good letters. I know that she wrote good letters. I know that I was an idiot, not really focused, not really paying attention.

We talked on the phone some nights until she fell asleep. I probably said "lasso the moon" drivel.

I drove Mr. Ford that summer, as he taught a full load of voice lessons, maybe even a busier summer than usual. His nickname was "Clarence". He gave nicknames to everyone except me. He could never think of a suitable nickname for me. Sometimes he tried Isa because I would say, "When I'sa kid", as in my very bad accent slurring "when I was" into "when I'zuh". Who can figure out how to spell that? And he tried mocking my middle name, Ainsworth. Heck, it was a weight, that family name, but it distinguished me from a zillion other David Cooks, so I used it, and have ever since. It isn't a bad name, stop making fun of it.

One day, when it was just too hot to turn right back around and go back for the Wednesday choir rehearsal at church, Mr. Ford sat in his kitchen, which I had never seen before, and loosened his necktie, another first sight.

"Open that bottom cabinet," he said. "Get out those plastic salad bowls and hand them to me."

They were nested like stacking blocks. He pulled something from deep in them and handed it to me.

It was a gray ceramic elephant that said "Germany" on its circus blanket.

"I've had that since I was a child. It's too small and not nice enough to be with the other figures in my collection." His apartment was lined with glass cases filled with fine porcelain and crystal.

He used to travel to collect antiques. That was how he had been paralyzed, in a car wreck in a rainstorm, driving back with a carload of antiques, ten years earlier.

"This little elephant belonged to a little girl that I knew in my hometown in Missouri when I was a boy. Gosh, I must have

272

been eight years old. I don't think I was smaller, because we played together for a few years, as I recall, but I couldn't have been any older than eight or nine because I remember that her mother taught us school one year, in first or second grade.

"Anyway, she died. And this is what I have to remember her." He closed his large hand over it and completely hid that elephant in the folds of his fingers.

"How did she die?" I asked.

"A horse kicked her in the head. I didn't even know she had a horse. I don't remember one. Back then I suppose a lot of people had horses. That was before the war. We were still in the Depression but, you know, to a little boy, life was just the same as it had always been. I remember going to her house, perhaps to see if she could come out and play, but the house was buzzing with people and there were cars and wagons and trucks all around, and I had to get past them to get to the house. There were white sheets hanging everywhere, like curtains. They must have tried to make it like a hospital, all very clean to keep the dust and flies away.

"They told me she had died. I was turning to leave when her mother stopped me. 'I want you to remember her,' she said. 'She would want you to remember, you were her favorite friend.' And then she handed me this and I've kept it ever since, in the Marines and through the war years, and teaching high schools and coming here to the college. I've never shown that to anyone before now, though; never told anyone that story. Better put it back."

Karen came back from the summer expecting to see me, to talk about our letters. But as soon as I saw her something flipped in my head.

The only way I can explain my attitude and my behavior is to bring up George Bailey from *It's a Wonderful Life* and the awful way he treated Mary Hatch (Donna Reed). That was what I was like and how I felt, I suddenly didn't want anyone to tell me what I wanted or who I loved or anything. I wanted to be my own man and make my own choices and I didn't want some fresh faced kid to keep me from heading off to the hill of my choice.

But I caused her to cry.

In short I was a stupid confused louse. I was going to tell the worst and stupidest story of how I treated her at Christmas – more accurately said is that I didn't treat her, I let her down – ugh. I guess I have to tell it. It went like this: I earned spending money through odd jobs and as it got into December and closer to Christmas it became more difficult to collect on those, running from this person to that one to remind them of ten dollars here and twenty dollars there. I wanted cash to buy Christmas presents and I became possessed of some notion that the presents had to be extra special and huge and somehow show off, and that some of them had to generously make up for past Christmases where I had been lacking. I sat behind her in choir rehearsals and I came in crowing one day because I had just collected the biggest debt, seventy-five dollars a doctor owed me for artwork, and I sat behind her and said, "Guess what I have? I've got Christmas money, I have. I'm going out to buy presents after this."

The next day was Thursday, I think, and I showed up for work at the desk of the college library only to find a plate full of my favorite cookies, chocolate chip meringue cookies, homemade and freshly baked, waiting for me. Karen had dropped them off. Oh, no, I knew what had happened.

Any sensible person would have begged, stolen or borrowed twenty dollars and run out and bought her some presents, but I was not sensible. My brain and heart obviously did not work right and had not for months. I called her and told her – yes, told her, as if confessing was the best way – I told her over the phone that I realized the she had misunderstood me and that I had not bought any presents for her. I am the louse that spoiled Christmas. And I know that I made her cry.

She was still determined through her tears and anger to believe that I loved her and cared about her and that I would one day realize that she was the right woman for me, the only woman, The Woman.

I talked to her almost every day, throughout the whole year. I walked her from the music building back to her dorm almost every night, even though it was my ridiculously busy senior year *and* I tried to date other girls to prove that she and I were really like friends and really like brother and sister, and yet I came back to her over and over, treating her like a little sister, as if she was helpless. She scoffed at that. She pointed out to me how I cared about her, was concerned about her, and that she knew I loved her and that she was the only girl for me. It was like that all year and even up to graduation.

I was Henry Ford's driver all that year. He and I sat in Primos Restaurant many afternoons and talked. I think he bought me many steak sandwiches. But my time as driver ended after the college year ended, as per the "tradition" he had established through ten years of hiring students from the choir to drive him.

After graduation in 1978 I looked for jobs. It went about the same way it had gone when I looked for jobs after high school. I still did the kind of spot work for cash that I had always done, cleaning Mr. Clark's gutters, repairing someone's cabinets, caulking someone else's windows, sweeping away pine straw, drawing, painting, lettering, making signs, whatever I could just so I had money in my pocket. I didn't have enough to make a checking account's fees worth having. I still lived in the house on Monroe Street with my mother.

In June or July, sometime in the summer, Karen asked me to go with her to the old silent film festival at the local Little Theatre. We saw "Wings" with live piano accompaniment. I had not seen her for weeks.

During those weeks away from me she had discovered her independence by taking drives with her younger sister Janet and exploring historic places. She cut her hair. She bought new clothes.

She had cut her hair quite short and it showed off the fine structure of her face. She seemed confident and self-possessed. I asked her how long she had planned that evening to the cinema, planned to ask me to go with her to see an old movie. She smiled and admitted that it had been weeks. I said that I supposed that she didn't trust me anymore, and she shook her head and said, no, she didn't, that it would take months, maybe years to regain trust after breaking up like that, after injuring her pride and turning on

278

her. I said I understood. I dropped her off at her brother's apartment where she stayed that summer, but as she stood in the doorframe, looking very much like a very real person yet at the same time like someone in a scene of a motion picture, really like Donna Reed in that Capra film, I said, "I guess you just won't give up and go away."

She asked me what I meant.

"You may not trust me any longer, and it may take me a long time to prove that I can be trusted, but I guess that you won't give up and you won't go away."

"I told you that I love you," Karen said. "I told you that I know that you love me, even if you don't know it, and I told you that I am the right woman for you and I always will be."

"I think you're right," I said.

I can remember dialogue from countless films and plays and books and I have poems memorized but I can't recall the exact words we said on the most important night of our lives that set in motion the next forty years. I can't remember, but I'm not going to make something up.

Whatever we said, we were going to be dating again, at least for a six month trial period.

I was like a sort of vagabond, I suppose, the unemployed graduate searching for a job.

I stayed in contact with Henry Ford through the summer. He sometimes needed a driver, although Gus Schreiber officially had that job for the next college year.

Then, in late September Clarence called and invited me to a party. He needed for me to drive him to it and expected Gus to drive him back. I may have that reversed, and my memory of walking to his apartment may be from another time and all backward, but considering what happened after that, such details can hardly matter.

Let's just imagine that I walked to Henry Ford's as I often did, and found him waiting in his wheelchair at his car, neatly dressed in a nice suit, as was his daily custom. We were going to Dr. Bill Cook's house, right across the street from the college. I pulled into their drive so that we could easily get the wheelchair into the house without climbing stairs.

It wasn't a Halloween party, not in late September. Maybe it was a Homecoming party, I just don't remember. It was forty years ago. It was a gathering.

I was standing behind Mr. Ford, holding the handles of his chair.

Suddenly, Mr. Ford's head dropped forward. Something was wrong.

"Henry! Clarence! Wake up!" Someone loosened his tie. "He isn't breathing."

Dr. Cook said, "We'll get him to the hospital. It will be faster if we go now, faster than an ambulance. I have a light." And by that he meant an emergency light on his car.

I held the handles of his chair and tilted it back, and we were quickly out of the house and heading down the front steps, down the hill, and someone was in front at his feet. It was a long way down that hill in the dark, a lot of steps. At the bottom was a station wagon with its engine running and the tailgate open. We hoisted Henry into the wagon, and then I heard it, a gurgling sound like a choking snore in his throat.

"That's the death rattle," the doctor said. I could tell even in the dark that he instantly regretted what he said. "We'll go to the hospital and we won't give up trying." They didn't think I should go along. The doors closed.

They drove away for the hospital and left me in the dark at the curb. I think I went back up and into the house. I think we stayed in touch with them by phone at the hospital. I think we prayed. But I don't remember when or how the last word came, or how each person turned to other things, to ending the evening and to be going on, going to whatever other cares and duties we had, or just going on back to our own homes.

I had one last duty, to park Mr. Ford's car at the college and give the keys to Tuna Waldron. He had been "Clarence's" driver before me, and he knew the family better than I did, and he lived in married housing on campus, so he was older and more suitable as the one to whom to entrust the keys.

I felt a sleepiness, a weary emptiness I had never felt before, as if I had been on watch for nights on end and my job was now over. I've experienced that same feeling many times since then, but that was the first time. It was as if I had really wanted to collapse earlier and had kept going not on strength but on determination, the determination to complete the last task with which I had been entrusted.

After I gave the keys to Tuna, in the black of night, I walked to Karen's dorm. Karen wanted to go with me to my house. I don't remember whether we drove there or walked there, neither does she, nor when and how I started crying but I started crying and I couldn't stop, great huge gasping sobs.

I was crying so hard that I started to vomit. All night I was racked by sobs and racked by vomiting. I'd never done that before and I've never done that since. I cried so loud and hard that I couldn't hear anything, and I vomited so loud and hard that the noise overwhelmed everything.

I guess Karen and my mother were worried and talked. I have no idea what time it was or how many hours that went on. After forty years, Karen can't remember, she just recalls my mother fretting and hovering, and letting her stay, and then letting Karen take over whatever care there was or vigil.

Karen was there when I woke up. She had kept watch until I fell asleep, I guess, or fallen asleep with me.

After the funeral I had taken Karen back to the campus. I knew that Henry's family would still be at his apartment and I wanted something. I wanted something to hold and remember him. I suppose that I wanted to always have proof that we had been friends. Karen got out at the music building and I drove on to the apartments.

Mr. Ford's sister remembered me. I asked her if I could

come inside and have some little thing of Mr. Ford's to remember

him. She looked at me a little warily. He had an expensive

collection of porcelain bric-a-brac, Wedgewood, and Blenheim and

Waterford crystal, and I suspect she wondered if I was about to

reach for something valuable. I went into the kitchen and opened

the bottom cupboard where the Tupperware mixing bowls nested.

Inside the smallest one was the little gray elephant, right where he

had placed it on the day he told me the story. Did he just own

kitchenware but never used it?

I held the little porcelain elephant in my hand and told

them the story as Henry had told it to me, about them being

friends as children, maybe eight or nine years old, in Missouri in the

early Thirties. They used to play together all the time, but one day

he had come to her farm house to find it swarming with people,

white bed sheets hung like curtains partitioning rooms. The girl's

mother had quietly told him that his friend the little girl had been

kicked in the head by a horse and had died. Before he turned to leave, the mother had given him the little elephant so that he had something to take with him so that he would remember her.

I looked at them, all quiet, it was obvious that they had never heard that story.

I put the elephant into my pocket and left to go back to the college campus and find Karen.

Karen was waiting at the music building. She had been talking to Lewis Dalvet, the conductor of the Mississippi Symphony Orchestra. She was still a student. It was only the beginning of October in her senior year. I had met her precisely two years before.

She met me at the base of the steps.

"Did you succeed?" she asked.

"I pulled something up from the past", I answered and showed her the little gray elephant in the palm of my hand.

She smiled. "Good. Did you tell them the story?"

"I did. None of them had ever heard it."

"We are going to get old together, you and I," she said. "I want to see you as an old man."

I had no imagination of that.

"I can't imagine you as an old woman."

"Just look at Grandma. Remember her photograph that I showed you?"

I remembered Grandpa Blake who seemed to me a bit shrunken and bent over.

"Why do the men always seem to shrink but women seem to stay about the same?" I remarked.

"That isn't going to happen. Don't be silly. I have to go practice, I still have classes."

"It's good to have work and a purpose, and your mind on the future."

An autumn breeze brushed her hair. She squeezed my hand and turned.

She walked into the music building to find a practice room.

Made in the USA
Coppell, TX
16 July 2021